89-0791

Smoking and the State

Smoking and the State

Social Costs, Rent Seeking, and Public Policy

Robert D. Tollison
George Mason University

Richard E. Wagner
George Mason University

Lexington Books

D. C. Heath and Company/Lexington, Massachusetts/Toronto

Library of Congress Cataloging-in-Publication Data
Smoking and the state.
Includes index.
1. Tobacco industry—Government policy—United
States. 2. Tobacco—Taxation—United States.
3. Smoking—United States. I. Tollison, Robert D.
II. Wagner, Richard E.
HD9136.S67   1988   362.2   87-45981
ISBN 0-669-17100-X (alk. paper)

Published simultaneously in Canada
Printed in the United States of America
International Standard Book Number: 0-669-17100-X
Library of Congress Catalog Card Number 87-45981

The paper used in this publication meets the minimum requirements of
American National Standard for Information Sciences—Permanence of
Paper for Printed Library Materials, ANSI Z39.48-1984. ∞™

89 90 91 92 8 7 6 5 4 3 2

Contents

List of Tables

Preface

Tobacco products are among the most highly taxed and strictly regulated products available to the American public. Moreover, Washington, D.C., and state capitals across the land annually witness a continual procession of proposals for still further taxation and regulation. Such proposals are supported by claims that smoking damages health—not just the health of smokers but the health of nonsmokers who are exposed to smokers' smoke. The health toll reportedly exacted by smoking, when reduced to economic terms, has been placed by some scholars as high as $100 billion, which is more than $3 per pack of cigarettes smoked.

Although many scientists believe that smoking harms health, many do not, or at least they believe that there is presently no valid scientific basis for accepting the hypothesis that smoking damages health over the hypothesis that it does not. There is continuing controversy within the scientific community about the effect of smoking on the health of smokers and nonsmokers. What some scholars see as strong data that smoking damages health, others see as a congeries of ambiguities and contradictions that makes it impossible to conclude that smoking does or does not damage health. The issues involved in assessing the alleged health consequences of smoking are numerous and complex, and any scientific consensus appears to lie some distance in the future.

We do not seek in this book to advance scientific discussion about the effect of smoking on health. We seek only to examine the economic consequences of smoking for nonsmokers. To this end, we accept for purposes of discussion the hypothesis that smoking damages health. Much of the literature on the social costs of smoking is based on the assumption that smoking has been proved to cause human disease and to be addictive. Since the purpose of this book is to analyze the scientific validity of the social cost literature, not to address the accuracy of those causal assumptions, we will use those same assumptions in our discussion of this issue. Our interest is in identifying just who bears whatever costs might be due to smoking. One polar possibility is that smokers themselves bear the full measure of such costs. The other polar possibility is that nonsmokers bear those costs. In this case, a $100 billion cost of smoking implies that, on average, smokers impose a cost of $500 on each nonsmoker in the nation—$2,000 for a nonsmoking family of four.

Depending on whether those costs are predominantly borne by smokers or by nonsmokers, very different implications for public policy surely arise. If smokers bear the costs of their smoking, we submit that little if any issue of public policy should arise, particularly within the normative framework of the American polity as constituting a free people. But if nonsmokers bear significant portions of those costs, tobacco taxation and regulation may be important instruments for making smokers more fully responsible for the costs of their smoking.

Although we are economists, we have written this book not just for economists but for everyone who is interested in possible public policy measures concerning smoking. In so doing, we have tried to limit our use of technical economic argumentation and concepts; where we could not avoid such usage, we have tried to present it in an understandable fashion to the layman.

The manuscript for this book was produced under a grant from the Tobacco Institute. We are grateful to Gary M. Anderson for research assistance. The views expressed are those of the authors and are not necessarily those of the Institute.

1
Smoking and the State:
An Overview

More than twenty years have now passed since the U.S. Surgeon General declared what many people had already believed for quite some time—that smoking could be hazardous to one's health. The Surgeon General has continued to issue reports on the hazards of smoking, and the World Health Organization has recently called smoking "the most important preventable health problem in the world." Similarly, in the 1985 report of the Office of Technology Assessment (OTA), *Smoking Related Deaths and Financial Costs*, smoking was held to be responsible for between 186,000 and 398,000 deaths in the United States in 1982; OTA's "best" estimate was 314,000. Moreover, it stands to reason that if smoking is an unhealthy activity, there is a cost in terms of illness, death, and medical care associated with smoking. The same OTA-sponsored study estimated that the annual cost in 1985 dollars of these health problems associated with smoking ranged from $40 billion to $100 billion in the United States; the "best" estimate was $65 billion, which is $2.17 per pack.

The ever-increasing fervor with which many people have joined the battle against smoking—as in supporting higher taxes on tobacco and more stringent restrictions on the ability of people to smoke—has surely been intensified by the belief that smoking exacts a high toll, both medically and economically. Surgeon General C. Everett Koop has articulated a vision of a smoke-free society, in which any remaining smokers could smoke only in the privacy of their homes and only in the company of other smokers. Like the lepers of old, smokers will be banished from the rest of society by the year 2000 if Surgeon General Koop's campaign is successful.

Government involvement with tobacco products is long-standing, widespread, expanding, and contentious. Taxes raise the price of cigarettes by about 50 percent in the United States, although there is variation from state to state because of differences in state taxes. Each year there are calls in various state legislatures for still further increases in tobacco taxes. The federal government doubled its tax on cigarettes to 16 cents per pack on a temporary basis in 1983 and made it permanent in 1985. A number of people have proposed to double it again, and some have even proposed to raise it to about $2 per pack. Moreover, there are a growing number of regulations concerning the advertising of tobacco products, their labeling, and where they can and cannot be smoked—with no end in sight, short of the disappearance of tobacco products.

Allegations about the harmful health effects of tobacco and the resulting costs to American society have been at the forefront of justifications for the escalating war on tobacco. In this book, we seek to assess these claims about the cost of smoking and to develop their implications, primarily for the nonsmoking majority of Americans. With respect to the $65 billion health cost of smoking noted earlier, for instance, we ask who in particular pays that bill. It is commonly said to be a cost to "society," but society cannot pay bills—only individuals can. We seek to examine whether the cost of smoking rests with smokers or with nonsmokers. If the $65 billion cost rests with the 50 million or so adult smokers, they are sacrificing, on average, $1,300 per year, in addition to the price of tobacco products, to satisfy their desire for those products. In a society that remains true to the foundations of the American Republic, however, the bearing of such costs would be the business of smokers, and few if any issues of public policy would arise.

But if, by contrast, that cost rests on the 100 million or so adult nonsmokers, they are sacrificing, on average, $650 per year to subsidize the damage that smokers inflict on themselves. To be sure, the American polity is replete with income and wealth transfers of all kinds, each of which involves one set of people gaining at the expense of others. Nonetheless, within the normative framework of the American Republic, there is a plausible basis for seeking to make smokers more fully bear the costs of their choice to smoke.

Our primary purpose in this book is to examine the various allegations about the costs of smoking, seeking to determine the extent to which they are borne by smokers themselves and the extent to which they are borne by nonsmokers. In so doing, we do not question the belief that smoking is harmful to health; we seek only to examine the extent to which the associated costs are split between smokers and nonsmokers.

Chapter 2 explores contrasting lines of argument concerning the taxation of tobacco products. Cigarettes are taxed about ten times as heavily as most other products that people consume. On top of this heavy tax discrimination, smoking is heavily concentrated among people with below-average incomes, so cigarette taxation is strongly regressive with respect to income. Such strongly regressive tax discrimination would generally encounter strong opposition among students and makers of tax policy. But there is little such opposition to be found when it comes to tobacco taxation. In part, this is because there are contrary lines of argument that can be used to support such discrimination in cases where use of the produce entails significant costs beyond those reflected in the market price of the product. In such cases, tobacco taxation would not be so much a form of discrimination as an instrument of justice or fairness.

In chapters 3 through 5, we examine the arguments and evidence regarding the social or external costs of smoking. Our central interest here lies in exploring the extent to which the $40 billion to $100 billion or so that is commonly portrayed as the annual cost of smoking is paid by smokers or by nonsmokers, taking it for granted that smoking has negative health consequences (if it did not, there would be no costs of smoking beyond those represented by the cost of producing cigarettes). In chapters 3 and 4, we examine the economic consequences of the harm that smokers inflict upon themselves; in chapter 5, we examine the economic consequences of the harm they are alleged to inflict upon others. Chapter 3 explores what are sometimes called the indirect costs of smoking. These are the costs in terms of increased sickness and earlier death and thus represent efforts to assess the costs of lost work and life. Chapter 4 examines the direct medical expenses of treating smokers. Chapter 5 considers the costs that smokers might impose on nonsmokers through damaging the nonsmokers' health—costs that have been in the forefront of many of the arguments for greater regulation of the places where people may or may not smoke.

One of the main contributions of the theory of public choice, which itself represents an effort to apply economic reasoning to political phenomena, has been a recognition that the production of public policy follows an economic logic and that the policy measures that are actually developed may sometimes bear little resemblance to measures that would be enacted under some reasonable concept of the public interest. Rather than acting to correct market failures, governments often act to create conditions leading to those failures. Moreover, there are understandable economic reasons why governments might act in this way. Chapter 6 explores the taxation and regulation of tobacco from such a public choice perspective, and chapter 7 sets forth some of the implications of our preceding analysis for public policy, both in particular regard to tobacco and in general regard to the operation and reform of the processes of policy formation within the present American polity.

2
Justice, Discrimination, and Tobacco Taxation

G overnments discriminate against smokers by taxing them substantially more heavily than they tax anyone else. The federal government taxes cigarettes at $8 per thousand, which is 16 cents per pack of twenty. All states tax cigarettes, at rates ranging from a low of 2 cents per pack in North Carolina to a high of 26 cents in Connecticut and Massachusetts. Moreover, state tax rates have been increasing sharply in recent years. As of 1984, cigarette taxes exceeded 20 cents per pack in twelve states, whereas only three states exceeded 20 cents in 1980. A majority of states, twenty-six, had cigarette tax rates in 1984 at least equal to the federal tax rate of 16 cents per pack, whereas only fourteen states could make that claim in 1980.[1] In a significant number of states, the combined federal and state tax on cigarettes is in the vicinity of 40 cents per pack. If a pack of cigarettes sells for $1.20 in such a state, the price net of tax is 80 cents. In such a case, the consumption of cigarettes is being taxed at 50 percent, which is about ten times as high as the tax rate imposed on most products under general sales taxation. There is a rather intense tax discrimination against cigarettes within our prevailing federal and state revenue systems.

Is there any justification, aside from political expediency or power, for such massive tax discrimination against the consumers of tobacco products, particularly in light of the limited revenues those taxes yield? A long tradition of tax analysis explains why tax discrimination is inequitable and inefficient: It is inequitable because it discriminates among people in the tax burdens they are asked to bear, merely because of differences in the things they choose to consume; and it is inefficient because it leads people to substitute lower-taxed, nontobacco items, which they value less, for higher-taxed, tobacco items, which they value more. The primary rebuttal to the claim that tobacco taxation is inequitable and inefficient is what economists refer to as *corrective taxation*. This term suggests that in some cases, what appears to be discriminatory taxation might actually be a means of offsetting other forms of inequity and inefficiency.

Inequity through Tobacco Tax Discrimination

Economists and philosophers have pondered the principles of just taxation for centuries and in the process have articulated two main principles: horizontal equity and vertical equity. Horizontal equity is a requirement that people who have the same income or wealth or expenditure, depending on which of these three categories forms the basis for taxation, should pay the same tax for the support of general government expenditures. It is unfair to tax some people more than others for the support of such expenditures simply because of differences in the sources of their income, the forms of their wealth, or the objects of their expenditure.

The taxation of cigarettes and other tobacco products creates horizontal inequity because people whose expenditures are the same pay different amounts of tax to support general government services, depending merely on the particular objects of their expenditure. A sales tax, by contrast, fulfills the requirement of horizontal equity: If you and your neighbor spend the same amount, you pay the same amount of tax. This happens because sales taxes are *general*, nondiscriminatory levies on all (or most) items of consumption, whereas excise taxes are discriminatory levies on *specific* items of consumption. People who spend the same amount pay different amounts of excise tax to finance general government services simply because of differences in the things they buy. People who smoke pay more than people who don't to support government services of general public benefit. Hence, smokers are taxed for the benefit of nonsmokers. Any excise tax, including the cigarette tax, is but the converse of a special tax privilege; it is a special *tax penalty* on a particular form of consumption. Whereas most items of consumption are taxed in the vicinity of 5 percent, cigarettes are approaching an average tax rate in the vicinity of 50 percent.

Excise taxes such as those on tobacco products also violate the principle of vertical equity. Unlike horizontal equity, which is conceptually sharp in that two people in the same economic position either do or do not pay the same taxes for the support of general government services, vertical equity is subject to some questions of interpretation on which scholars differ.[2] Nearly all scholars agree that vertical equity is violated when people with lower incomes or expenditures are taxed at higher rates than people with higher incomes for the support of general government services. Disagreement about vertical equity begins to emerge when an effort is made to go beyond this essentially negative injunction that tax rates should not rise as income or expenditure falls—an injunction that is consistent with constant or flat tax rates—to a positive statement that tax rates should rise by some particular amount as income or expenditure rises. It is generally agreed that regressive taxation violates vertical equity; it is not generally agreed that vertical equity requires a particular form of progressive taxation over proportional or flat-rate taxation.

Tobacco taxation violates the most generally accepted formulation of vertical equity, for it imposes a higher rate of tax on people with lower incomes or expenditures than it imposes on people with higher incomes. The share of their incomes that smokers spend on cigarettes generally falls as income rises. For this reason, the tobacco tax is a highly regressive levy. For instance, according to a 1981 survey, households in the lowest income quintile spent an average of 2.3 percent of their income on tobacco products, while households in the highest income quintile spent an average of 0.42 percent of their income on tobacco products (U.S. Department of Labor, 1983, p. 54). This point is illustrated by table 2–1, with reference to three hypothetical smokers. This table conveys the point that smokers spend more on tobacco as their incomes rise, but that the share of income spent on tobacco falls as income rises. When the amount of tobacco tax is expressed as a share of income (in the last column), the tax rate falls in half as income rises from

Table 2–1
Illustration of the Regressivity of Tobacco Taxation

Income	Tobacco Purchases	Purchases/Income	Tobacco Tax[a]	Tax/Income
$10,000	$200	2.0%	$ 66.67	0.667%
$20,000	280	1.4%	93.33	0.467%
$30,000	300	1.0%	100.00	0.333%

[a] Our basic illustration of the cigarette tax, as explained in the text, is that it raises the price of cigarettes by 50 percent, from $0.80 to $1.20 per pack. This means that tobacco taxes constitute one-third of expenditures on tobacco.

$10,000 to $30,000. Furthermore, the use of tobacco products declines as income rises, thereby strengthening the portrait of regressivity. Although about one-third of the adult population smokes, smokers are not equally represented at all income levels. They are more heavily represented at lower-income levels, as table 2–2 illustrates.

    Vertical and horizontal equity are principles derived from the financing of expenditures of general public benefit. Horizontal equity acts as a protection against the discriminatory imposition of tax burdens upon a subset of people for the benefit of all. It is surely an understandable reflection of human nature that there might be much support for such tax discrimination as tobacco taxation represents. Only about one-third of adults smoke—and who wouldn't prefer that someone else pay taxes that he or she might otherwise have to pay? Furthermore, smoking is particularly unpopular among the various elites in society; smoking is predominantly an activity of the working classes, not the professional

Table 2–2
The Declining Frequency of Smoking as Income Rises

Income Class	Adult Population	Regular Smokers	Percentage of Smokers
Under $7,000	26,227,396	8,650,224	32.98
$7,000–$14,999	38,478,567	13,290,912	34.54
$15,000–$24,999	37,245,561	12,128,637	32.56
Over $25,000	46,772,615	13,828,855	29.57

Source: Calculated from William F. Shughart II and James M. Savarese, "The Incidence of Taxes on Tobacco," in Robert D. Tollison (ed.), *Smoking and Society: Toward a More Balanced Assessment* (Lexington, Mass.: Lexington Books, 1986), pp. 291–92.

classes in society. For instance, in their study of the prevalence of smoking by occupational category, Sterling and Weinkam (1976) reported that among men, 30 percent of lawyers smoke whereas 60 percent of garage laborers smoke. They similarly reported that among women, 20 percent of schoolteachers smoke whereas 50 percent of waitresses smoke.

The one case in which discriminatory taxation might not violate horizontal equity is where the tax revenues are used not to finance expenditures of general benefit but to finance expenditures of particular benefit to the people who are being taxed. The gasoline tax, when it is used to finance highways, is a good illustration of this point. People differ in their use of highways; some drive extensively, and some do not drive at all. The use of a gasoline tax to finance highways is a way of approximating a system of charging people for their use of highways. The users of highways could, of course, be charged directly for their usage, as they are on toll roads. But it would be prohibitively expensive to set up toll booths on city streets. Although a gasoline tax is not identical to a system of direct charging, it is a reasonable approximation and one that, administratively, is much less costly to operate.

Whether tobacco taxation is a reasonable means of financing government services that are provided to smokers but not to others is something we shall explore later in this chapter and elsewhere in this book. Some people have advocated that the cigarette tax be earmarked for the support of Medicare, under the argument that smokers impose particularly heavy burdens upon Medicare; we shall examine this argument in chapter 4.[3] In the absence of some sound basis for thinking that tobacco taxation is a means of charging particular beneficiaries for particular services they receive—services that are not available to the general public—specific excise taxes have little to recommend them. They are a form of tax discrimination, of a highly regressive form, that taxes particular sets of people for the general benefit. The interests of equity and efficiency are better served by using broad, general taxes to finance services of general benefit and by reserving specific excises and fees to finance services that benefit specific sets of people who use the services those taxes and fees help to finance.

Inefficiency through Tobacco Taxation

The roughly $10 billion that various governments in the United States collect from excise taxes on tobacco products is generally paid for by consumers of those products, whose disposable incomes are reduced by $10 billion by the tax. However, the burden that an excise tax imposes on consumers will typically *exceed* the amount of revenue that governments collect. This additional burden is referred to by economists as *excess burden*.

Suppose that in the absence of a cigarette tax, cigarettes would sell for 80 cents per pack and people would buy 32 billion packs per year.[4] One of the central features of a competitive market economy is that the price of a product tends to equal its cost of production. Moreover, the cost of producing a product tends, in turn, to equal the value consumers place on the other products that were forgone to produce the product in question. To say that the cost of producing a pack of cigarettes is 80 cents, then, is equivalent to saying that the value of the other output that could have been produced had the cigarettes not been produced instead is itself worth 80 cents to consumers.[5] Therefore, in the absence of an excise tax in a competitive economy, the price that consumers may pay for one product is equal to the value they place on the alternative output that could have been produced by the resources that were used, instead, to produce the product in question. It is impossible to rearrange the pattern of production to increase the value of what is produced. Any such rearrangement would substitute lower-valued for higher-valued output and, hence, would be inefficient.

Now consider the imposition of an excise tax on cigarettes of 40 cents per pack, which raises the price to $1.20 per pack. Suppose that consumers respond to the rise in price by reducing their purchases to 28 billion packs per year.[6] Consumers must now pay $1.20 for cigarettes, while the cost of the cigarettes, which is equivalent to the value of the output they must sacrifice to get the additional cigarettes, remains at 80 cents. The key to excess burden resides in this divergence between price and cost that the excise tax creates.

After the tax is imposed, consumers pay $1.20 for a pack of cigarettes that costs, in terms of alternative output that must be forgone to produce the cigarettes, only 80 cents. This situation means that the value to consumers of an additional pack of cigarettes is $1.20, whereas the value of whatever other output they would have to give up to get those additional cigarettes is only 80 cents. Consumers would be better off by a shift of resources into the production of cigarettes until output increases sufficiently to lower the price that people would be willing to pay for cigarettes to 80 cents. The excise tax makes consumers worse off—beyond the $11.2 billion tax extraction that results from the 40 cent per pack tax on 28 billion packs—by the extent to which the value they place on additional cigarettes exceeds the cost of producing those additional cigarettes. This magnitude is the excess burden of the excise tax; in the presence of such a tax, people are led to buy less of the product than that which would maximize the satisfaction they get from their expenditures as consumers.

It is possible to assess empirically the extent of the excess burden of any particular excise tax. A simple approximation of this magnitude is the change in price brought about by the tax, multiplied by the resulting change in the consumption of cigarettes. In the illustration at hand, the excess burden, EB, is

$$EB = .5 \times \$0.40 \times 4 \text{ billion} = \$800 \text{ million}$$

In this case, the excess burden, which is a measure of the waste associated with the use of the selective excise tax, is more than 7 percent of the revenues the government collects. For each dollar the government collects in tax, consumers of cigarettes lose $1.07—$1 of which is collected by government and $0.07 of which simply evaporates, as it were, because the tax induces a shift of resources away from the production of products consumers value more highly into the production of products they value less highly. Tobacco taxes are not only regressive and discriminatory levies but also wasteful. Tobacco taxation would seem to fare quite poorly by standard norms of equity, justice, and efficiency.

Tobacco Taxation as Corrective Taxation

Although normative statements of tax principles have generally been hostile to excise taxation, particularly as an instrument of general-fund financing, there is one principled line of support for excise taxation: An excise tax can serve as an indirect way of charging for resources that are used in producing a product when the costs of those resources are not reflected in the price of that product. In such cases, the very raison d'être of an excise tax is its ability to discriminate among types of consumption, thereby reducing the amount people consume of the taxed products or possibly altering some of the characteristics or attributes of those products. The rationalization for the imposition of a selective excise tax on the consumers of particular products—as against imposing burdens on the general class of consumers—revolves around the possibility that, in some cases, the market price of a product may not fully reflect its true cost of production. In such cases, the true cost of a product will exceed the price consumers have to pay for it. These omitted or neglected aspects of cost are commonly referred to as *external costs,* to indicate that they are costs that are not reflected in the normal market transactions between buyers and sellers.

With respect to cigarettes, 80 cents may reflect the cost of such resources as the tobacco, paper, warehousing, shipping, and so on, that go into the production of cigarettes. When someone pays 80 cents for a pack of cigarettes, that payment will compensate the owners of the resources that were used in producing the cigarettes. However, many people argue that there is a cost of smoking, and of tobacco consumption generally, that goes beyond the direct costs of production and represents such factors as the added medical expenses that smokers incur because of their impaired health due to smoking, their diminished contribution to economic life because they are sick more often and die sooner because they smoke, and the pain and suffering they impose on loved ones because of that sickness and death. As we will examine in detail in chapters 3 through 5, the pursuit of such arguments places the external cost of consuming tobacco products somewhere between $40 billion and $100 billion annually. If these figures and their interpretation are accurate, the price of cigarettes falls short of the cost of smoking, and covering that cost would require a cigarette tax in the vicinity of $2 per pack, which would correspond to an external cost of about $60 billion for 30 billion packs.

The central idea of corrective taxation is to impose a tax equal to the external cost associated with the consumption of a particular product. If this is not done, there is actually an excess burden from the failure to do so. The argument on this point is symmetrical with the discussion of the excess burden of an excise tax that was presented earlier. In the absence of cigarette taxes, consumers would buy 32 billion packs of cigarettes per year at a price of 80 cents per pack. But suppose that the external cost of cigarette consumption is $1.60 per pack. The sacrifice of other output that results from the consumption of 32 billion packs of cigarettes would be $76.8 billion ($2.40 × 32 billion). Of this amount, smokers would pay only one-third—$25.6 billion. The remaining $51.2 billion represents the external cost of smoking, for each of the 32 billion packs that smokers smoke would carry an external cost of $1.60.

By reducing the consumption of cigarettes below 32 billion packs, alternative output valued at $2.40 would be acquired by sacrificing something worth only $0.80. The reduction in tobacco consumption would offer such a gain until people came to value their diminished quantity of cigarettes at $2.40 per pack. To illustrate this point, suppose that cigarettes were worth $2.40 per pack and only 20 billion packs were available per year. Smokers would pay $48 billion per year ($2.40 × 20 billion packs) for cigarettes. Of this amount, producers would receive $16 billion ($0.80 × 20 billion) as payment for tobacco, paper, and the like, and the government would collect $32 billion ($1.60 × 20 billion) in tax, presumably to serve as compensation for the external costs stemming from smoking. The gain that would result from the removal of this excess burden, and which would be made possible by the corrective tax, would be approximately $9.6 billion, computed by the formula:

$$\text{Welfare gain} = .5 \times \$1.60 \times 12 \text{ billion}$$

Principle versus Reality in Tobacco Taxation

To argue that if producers are able to ignore some costs of their production, a *properly* chosen tax will lead them to make the same choices regarding production that they would make if they took those costs directly into account is, of course, a truism. However, it does not follow that the actual imposition of an excise tax for what might seem to be corrective purposes will actually perform in the desired manner. Two types of issues arise regarding the application of ideas of external cost and corrective taxation to the consumption of tobacco products. One concerns the accuracy of the various estimates of disease and premature death that are commonly attributed to smoking. The other concerns the circumstances under which these costs, assuming that the diseases have been properly attributed to smoking, might properly be said to be external or uncompensated, as against being internal or personal. Even if it is accepted that smoking harms health, it does not follow that the disease, death, and medical expenses that are thus attributed to smoking represent an external or uncompensated cost and, thus, a drain on the economic well-being of the general members of society, as against being a cost to the individual smokers—a cost they have chosen to bear in exchange for the benefit they derive from smoking. In chapters 3 through 5, we shall explore the extent to which smokers and nonsmokers bear the costs that might stem from any diminished health due to smoking.

The abstract theory of corrective taxation is generally simpler than the reality such efforts at taxation address. Even in a world of benevolence, in which tax policy could be described as reflecting a single-minded devotion to the implementation of principles of corrective taxation, a difficult question of knowledge would have to be overcome concerning the formation of a correct, or even a reasonably informed, judgment of external cost. A market system generally produces such knowledge as a by-product of its internal operation. For instance, a failure by a firm to cover its cost of production means that the value consumers place on its output is less than the value they place on the alternative output that was sacrificed to produce the product in question. And the converse conclusion can be reached in the case of a firm that makes a profit.

But when a direct market test is absent, as is necessarily the case with external costs—for the very concept implies that some aspects of resource usage are not reflected in market transactions—the problem of securing knowledge is more difficult.

Moreover, a market system provides a strong incentive for people to make choices knowledgeably, because poor choices will result in losses. A growing body of contemporary literature on political economy and public choice has explained why political incentives often operate less strongly than market incentives to promote economic efficiency. In politics, the costs and gains of accurate or inaccurate choices are concentrated less strongly on those who make those choices, because more of those costs and gains are diffused generally throughout the citizenry. The loss from a governmental choice that is more costly than it need be is spread over all taxpayers, rather than being concentrated on those responsible for making that choice.

The principle of corrective taxation does not explain the actual practice of excise taxation. A particular tax may be rationalized on corrective grounds, but the reality of the situation might clash with that rationalization, possibly because the tax does not address accurately the nature of the external costs, or possibly because the alleged external costs are insignificant or even nonexistent. The real reason for the tax or regulatory measure may be a transfer of wealth. Tobacco taxation may be imposed not as a way of correcting for market failures that result because smokers do not pay the full costs associated with their smoking, but as a way of transferring tax burdens away from nonsmokers. There is growing recognition, stemming from the literature on public choice processes, that actual tax policies may be adopted for quite different reasons than the justifications commonly advanced in their support. For instance, the imposition of excise taxes on products consumed by a minority is a way of transferring income tax burdens, particularly if the taxed items have inelastic demands.

Considerations of political interest often dominate principles of corrective taxation in explaining the use of excise taxation. Excise taxes have commonly been levied on imported goods because the entry of goods from foreign countries generally funnels through ports or along certain highways, which makes such goods comparatively easy to tax. They have also been levied on goods that dominant groups in society either disapprove of or consume relatively slightly. Much of such excise taxation has been referred to as *sumptuary taxation*. This label has been applied to taxes on tobacco, liquor, playing cards, theater admissions, musical instruments, cameras, jewelry, furs, and pool tables, among numerous other items that have at one time been taxed or are now being taxed. This form of taxation essentially represents a transfer of income from less powerful classes of consumers, who pay higher taxes, to more powerful classes, who pay lower taxes.

One particularly sharp example of the possible cleavage between public-interest justifications commonly advanced for particular tax measures and the reality of those measures arises with regard to various proposals to earmark tobacco tax revenues for Medicare. It is a simple matter to incorporate tax earmarking into the theory of corrective taxation. This can be done by looking upon earmarking as a type of liability payment for damages done; the tax serves as an assessment of damages, and the earmarking of the revenues directs them to where the damages were inflicted.

The case for earmarking tobacco tax revenues for Medicare obviously assumes that smoking causes an increase in medical claims by people aged sixty-five and over. But even if it is assumed that smoking reduces health and increases medical expenses, it does not follow that the earmarking of a tax on tobacco to support Medicare is a reasonable substitute for direct user pricing as a means of getting smokers to pay for the excess costs of their smoking. This might be so if Medicare were truly an insurance program. However, Medicare, like all of the Social Security programs, is a welfare program, not an insurance program.[7] This characteristic of Medicare invalidates the argument that earmarking the tobacco tax for Medicare is a reasonable substitute for user pricing. If Medicare were truly an insurance program, people would pay directly, through their premiums, for their anticipated use of medical resources, and there would be no need for such an indirect method of pricing as tax earmarking.

Despite the widespread recognition in the scholarly community that Medicare, as well as the other Social Security programs, is essentially a welfare program, not an insurance program, there seems to be a substantial public belief that people do pay into genuine insurance programs with the various Social Security programs. The maintenance of the appearance of a contributory insurance system seems to be important in maintaining public support for Medicare, as well as for the other Social Security programs. The proposal to earmark tobacco taxes for the Medicare portion of Social Security seems well suited to satisfy those political objectives. To the extent that such earmarking can be made to appear reasonable as simply a type of contribution for particular services rendered to smokers, earmarking seems more likely to strengthen public support for Medicare than what would be likely to happen under general-fund financing. Earmarking cigarette taxes for Medicare, then, is perhaps seen more appropriately as part of a political strategy for collecting taxes than as one aspect of bringing contractual principles more fully into Medicare by trying to implement user pricing.

Notes

1. For a compendium of information on tobacco taxation, see Tobacco Institute (1985).
2. For a careful description of vertical equity and horizontal equity, see Musgrave (1959), chapters 5 and 8, respectively.
3. For a sample of proposals to earmark the cigarette tax for Medicare, consult various statements in Committee on Ways and Means (1986).
4. In illustrating a number of points about tobacco taxation, we shall adopt a "standard case" in which the tax is 40 cents per pack and the price of cigarettes in the absence of tax is 80 cents. Although such a standard case cannot fit every case perfectly, it is accurate in the central idea it portrays.
5. This point is explained clearly in Buchanan (1969).
6. This assumes a price elasticity of demand for cigarettes of −.33. For a summary of elasticity estimates, see Lewit and Coate (1982).
7. See, for instance, Ferrara (1980), Robertson (1981), and Weaver (1982).

3
Smoking and the Cost of Lost Production

A s noted in chapter 1, a recent survey sponsored by the Office of Technology Assessment placed the alleged social costs of smoking between $39 billion and $96 billion for 1985 and went on to postulate a "best" estimate of $65 billion, which is $2.17 per pack of cigarettes. About one-third of this cost was attributed to the medical expenses incurred by smokers, and the remaining two-thirds was attributed to the lost production that resulted from the increased rate of disease and death claimed to be associated with smoking. This chapter describes and assesses the estimation of the social costs of lost production attributed to smoking; the next chapter does the same assessment for the costs of medical care.

Smoking and Health: Common Allegations

The central logic behind the construction of estimates for the costs of smoking is simple and straightforward, even if the actual implementation of that logic is fraught with difficulties. The presumption that smoking damages health is the point of departure of any effort to assess the social cost of smoking, for if this presumption is invalid, there is no point in talking about any cost of smoking beyond the cost of producing and distributing cigarettes. Although a number of diseases have been associated statistically with smoking, the three diseases that have dominated the analysis of the health consequences of smoking are lung cancer, cardiovascular disease, and chronic obstructive lung disease (bronchitis and emphysema).

The first step in any effort to estimate the cost of smoking is to estimate the extent to which smoking harms health, for the "cost of smoking" represents merely the placement of a valuation upon "the health impairment caused by smoking." If smoking did not cause any such impairment, it would be nonsensical to speak of the "cost of smoking." Despite numerous difficulties in attempting to estimate the extent to which smoking impairs health, the principle behind the construction of such an estimate is a simple one. Any such effort at construction is grounded upon a comparison of the health characteristics of smokers and nonsmokers, attributing any differences in health characteristics between the two sets of people to smoking.

Suppose that a sample of 2,000 people is split evenly between smokers and nonsmokers. These people should be identical in all respects, except that 1,000 of them are smokers. This supposition means that they would all be of the same age, have the same occupational characteristics, possess the same genetic inheritances, and so on. To the extent that this supposition is correct, it seems reasonable to attribute the differential health patterns between the two sets of people to smoking and other behavioral characteristics. For instance, suppose that 50 of the 1,000 nonsmokers are hospitalized for 30 days each with cardiovascular disease and 100 of the 1,000 smokers are so hospitalized. Under the presumption that it is reasonable to attribute the excess cases of hospitalization beyond that experienced by the nonsmokers to smoking, 1,500 days of hospital care (50 excess cases at 30 days each) would be attributed to smoking's negative effect on health.

Whether such a supposition is correct, however, is at the center of the controversy over efforts to assess the health consequences of smoking. For instance, in his study of the effect of smoking on heart disease, Carl Seltzer (1980) found that "ex-smokers showed statistically significant differences from smokers who continued the habit in a number of cardiovascular symptoms, socio-personal characteristics, and metabolic and miscellaneous traits," meaning that "ex-smokers are not a representative sample of smokers with regard to their CHD-related characteristics or the extent of the smoking habit" (p. 276). What this means is that a statistical finding that ex-smokers have less heart disease than smokers does not by itself make it possible to infer that the cessation of smoking among those who would otherwise continue to smoke will reduce their likelihood of heart disease, because the ex-smokers may have had characteristics that would have led to less heart disease in the first place, even if they had continued to smoke.

In estimating the costs of the negative health consequences of smoking, it is common to distinguish between direct and indirect costs. Direct costs are the various excess medical expenses that are associated with smoking. In the foregoing illustration, they would be the medical costs of 1,500 days of hospital care plus whatever other medical services were involved in treating those people. Indirect costs are the lost production that results because people cannot work when they are hospitalized or miss work because of illness even when they are not hospitalized. Thus, in attempting to estimate the economic costs of smoking, it is necessary to start with an effort to gauge the health consequences of smoking and, from that point of departure, to make an inference about the resulting reduction in labor force participation. Once this physical description of how smoking affects health and labor force participation has been constructed, it is possible to attempt to estimate the cost of smoking.

Death from smoking is treated in essentially the same manner as illness caused by smoking. If 20 of the 1,000 nonsmokers die from cardiovascular disease during the year and 30 of the 1,000 smokers die from such disease, it is reasonable to attribute the 10 additional deaths beyond those suffered by the nonsmokers to smoking—because 20 of the smokers presumably would have died even if they did not smoke.[1] In the case of the 10 who died, the lost production is treated simply as an illness that lasts until retirement. If it is presumed that these 10 smokers would have retired at age sixty-five and if their average age at death was fifty-five, it is reasonable to attribute to smoking the loss of 100 years of production from these people.

In practice, of course, there is considerable room for differing judgments about those magnitudes. In part, this is because of differences in the extent to which negative health consequences are attributed to smoking. As table 3–1 shows, the Office of Technology Assessment attributed between 89,000 and 174,000 cancer deaths

Table 3–1
Smoking-Related Deaths, 1982

Disease	Number of Deaths (range)	"Best" Estimate	Life-Years Lost
Cancer	89,000–174,000	139,000	
Cardiovascular	48,000–170,000	123,000	
Chronic lung	49,000– 54,000	52,000	
Total	186,000–398,000	314,000	5,300,000

Source: Office of Technology Assessment, *Smoking-Related Deaths and Financial Costs* (Washington, D.C.: Office of Technology Assessment, 1985), p. 2.

in 1982 to smoking, with a "best" estimate of 139,000.[2] Similarly, between 48,000 and 170,000 cardiovascular disease deaths were attributed to smoking, with a "best" estimate of 123,000. For the three primary disease categories, the range of deaths attributed to smoking was 186,000 to 398,000, with a "best" estimate of 314,000.

Economic Assessment of Lost Production

Once such a description of the health consequences of smoking has been developed, the economic significance of those consequences can be assessed. Again, the underlying principles are simple, even if the actual practice is not. Consider the foregoing illustration in which 1,500 days of hospital care and ten deaths were attributed to smoking. What is needed to arrive at an economic assessment is some way of placing valuations on those health consequences. Suppose that the daily cost of hospital care is $400. If so, the medical costs associated with the excess hospitalization incurred by smokers would be $600,000. The cost of physicians' care and the medical costs associated with death could be estimated in similar fashion.

The estimation of the economic costs of lost production is equally simple in principle. Suppose that the people whose 1,500 days of hospitalization were attributed to smoking missed 2,400 days of work because of their illnesses. If those people had an average wage rate of $100 per day, it would be relatively straight-forward to evaluate the lost production resulting from their illnesses at $240,000. Not all illnesses result in hospitalization, of course, so additional sources of lost production due to smoking-related illnesses would have to be taken into account. Nonetheless, the central idea behind estimating the indirect costs of smoking-related illnesses is simply to derive, first, an estimate of the health consequences of smoking and, from this estimate, to develop an evaluation of the resulting reduction in labor force participation. This involves, first of all, an effort to construct a description of the ways in which the health of smokers differs from the health of *otherwise identical* nonsmokers in terms of deaths, illnesses, and lost work. From this description of consequences, an evaluation can be constructed according to the central principles just described.

Several people have tried to estimate the morbidity costs of smoking. For instance, M.H. Peston (1971) estimated that the annual cost of lost production attributable to smoking in Great Britain was £290 million. To construct this figure, he first estimated that 50 million days of work were missed because of illness attributed to smoking. After further estimating that the average daily wage rate of those ill workers was £5.8, he computed the estimated total amount of lost production to be £290 million. For the United States, Luce and Schweitzer (1978) estimated the cost of lost production attributed to smoking-related morbidity at $19.1 billion in 1976. If this amount were restated in 1985 dollars, Luce and Schweitzer's estimate for the United States would have been about $36 billion, which is more than one dollar per pack of cigarettes. Similarly, Kristein (1977) estimated those costs at $15.1 billion in 1975, which would extrapolate to about $30 billion in 1985 dollars.

The mortality attributed to smoking was treated in these studies as equivalent to morbidity that lasts until retirement. So the death of a fifty-five-year-old that was attributed to smoking was treated as if that person had suffered a permanently incapacitating illness or injury at that same age. If the work year for such a person was 250 days, and if the daily wage rate was $100, one year's lost work would be valued at $25,000. If this $25,000 annual figure were simply repeated each year until retirement, and if the retirement age were 65, the cost of the lost production that would be attributed to smoking would be $250,000.

Two types of complications arise in this case. One is the possibility that earnings will be higher or lower in future years. The other is the need to recognize that a dollar to be received next year is worth less now than a dollar to be received now. The reason is that a dollar to be received now can earn interest, so it is worth more than a dollar to be received one year from now. Alternatively, some amount less than one dollar held now can be converted into a dollar in one year. For instance, at a 10 percent rate of interest and in the absence of compounding, 91 cents now can be converted into a dollar in one year. Hence, a dollar to be received in one year is equivalent to only 91 cents now, at an interest rate of 10 percent. Although it is not necessary to go into the principles or mechanics of present value discounting here, it should be noted that estimation of the mortality costs of smoking, as contrasted to the morbidity costs, does involve such present value discounting.

The aforementioned authors who developed estimates of the morbidity costs of smoking also developed estimates of the mortality costs, expressing these costs in present value terms. With respect to Great Britain, Peston estimated the present value of the cost of death before the age of sixty-five at £150 million per year. He based this calculation on the presumption that there are 23,000 deaths before retirement that could be attributed to smoking each year, with the average length of time remaining before retirement being four years. The average present value of such a death was estimated at £6,400, giving a total cost of mortality of £147 million. For the United States, Luce and Schweitzer estimated the lost-production cost of smoking-related mortality at $12.3 billion for 1976, which in terms of the deflated value of the dollar a decade later would have been about $23 billion.

Because different approaches to the estimation of the health consequences of smoking will generate different attributions of smoking-related deaths and diseases, the estimated cost of medical care and lost production will also differ, even if there is no disagreement regarding the appropriate values to place on illness and lost production. The presence of disagreement about the valuation of such events would increase the range of cost estimates. As table 3–2 shows, Office of Technology Assessment estimates of the health care costs attributed to smoking in 1985 ranged from

Table 3–2

Costs of Smoking, 1985

Category	Cost Range		"Best" Estimate	
	Total	Per Pack	Total	Per Pack
Health care	$12–$35 billion	$ .38–$1.17	$22 billion	$ .72
Lost production	$27–$61 billion	$ .90–$2.02	$43 billion	$1.45
Total	$38–$95 billion	$1.27–$3.17	$65 billion	$2.17

Source: Office of Technology Assessment, *Smoking-Related Deaths and Financial Costs*, (Washington, D.C.: Office of Technology Assessment, 1985), p. 4.

$12 billion to $35 billion, with a "best" estimate of $22 billion. Similarly, the estimated cost of lost production ranged from $27 billion to $61 billion for 1985, with a "best" estimate of $43 billion. The range of cost estimates is obviously quite wide; the high estimate for total costs of smoking is 2.5 times as large as the low estimate. The width of this range attests to the difficulties of application in moving from the simple conceptual idea to the construction of actual estimates. But in any event, the magnitudes are quite large, ranging on a per pack basis from $1.27 to $3.17. If cigarettes presently sell for around $1 per pack, the full cost of smoking would seem to range from approximately $2 to $4 per pack.

Smoking and Workplace Efficiency

The argument that smoking entails a cost in terms of lost production is sometimes represented by the charge that smoking reduces workplace efficiency. Lost production and workplace efficiency are largely images of one another; attributing lost production to the damaged health of smokers must mean that the workplaces throughout the nation produce less than they would otherwise have produced. And beyond this lost production, it is sometimes claimed that smokers also increase such costs as maintenance and the replacement of furniture. Although the significance of these other costs has been shown to be dubious, the matter of absenteeism is worth further consideration.[3] Table 3–3 summarizes aggregate nationwide data on work loss by smokers and nonsmokers for 1970

Table 3–3

Smoking and Days of Lost Work Annually

				Current Smokers		
	Everyone	Never Smoked	Former Smokers	All	1–14 Cigarettes	15–24 Cigarettes	25 and More Cigarettes
1970							
Male	5.0	3.7	5.1	5.8	6.0	5.2	6.4
Female	5.9	5.1	5.3	7.4	7.1	7.9	7.2
1976							
Male	5.0	4.3	5.7	5.2	2.6	5.9	5.7
Female	5.8	5.1	6.3	6.6	6.2	5.7	9.3

Source: For 1970, U.S. Bureau of the Census, *Statistical Abstract of the United States: 1975* (Washington, D.C.: U.S. Government Printing Office, 1975), p. 90. For 1976, U.S. Bureau of the Census, Statistical Abstract of the United States: 1980 (Washington, D.C.: U.S. Government Printing Office, 1980), p. 130.

and 1976. A comparison of the columns labeled "Never Smoked" and "Current Smokers—All" conveys the impression that smokers are absent from work more often than nonsmokers. For 1970, nonsmoking men missed 2.1 fewer days of work than smoking men; nonsmoking women missed 2.3 fewer days than smoking women. Stated differently, the rate of absenteeism was nearly 60 percent higher among smoking men than among nonsmoking men. And among women, smokers were absent 45 percent more often than nonsmokers. For 1976, nonsmoking men missed 0.0 fewer days than smoking men, while nonsmoking women missed 1.5 fewer days than smoking women. In this case, smoking men were absent over 20 percent more often than nonsmoking men, while smoking women were absently nearly 30 percent more often than nonsmoking women.

Although these pieces of data conform to the impression that smokers are less healthy than nonsmokers and so miss more work, there are also some pieces of data in table 3–3 that do not conform to that impression, particularly the 1976 data. Although current smokers, on average, miss more work than people who never smoked, men who currently smoke, on average, miss less work than men who formerly smoked. Moreover, men who currently smoke fewer than fifteen cigarettes daily miss nearly two fewer days of work per year than men who never smoked. And women who currently smoke up to 24 cigarettes per day miss less work than women who formerly smoked. So the data on smoking and workplace absenteeism do not tell an unambiguous tale of smoking leading to increased sickness and absenteeism; different tales can be told, depending on how the data are aggregated and categorized.

More than this, it is questionable whether these data are, on balance, revealing or concealing. There are grounds for suggesting that data such as those in table 3–3 may mislead more than they inform. Many of those data give the impression that smokers miss more work than their nonsmoking co-workers. But this may be a false impression created by aggregation. Smokers are more heavily represented in blue-collar occupations than in white-collar occupations and professions, where nonsmokers predominate. This is illustrated by table 3–4. Among males, a majority of cooks, painters, mechanics, and others smoke, whereas less than one-third of engineers, lawyers, and accountants smoke. And among females, nearly half of waitresses, shipping clerks, and assemblers smoke, whereas less than a quarter of medical technicians, schoolteachers, and librarians smoke.

Yet white-color jobs themselves are generally more enjoyable

Table 3–4

Percentage of Smokers by Occupation

Men		Women	
Occupation	*% Smokers*	*Occupation*	*% Smokers*
Garage laborers	58.5	Waitresses	49.6
Cooks	57.5	Shipping and receiving clerks	48.5
Maintenance painters	56.3	Assemblers	43.6
Pressmen and plateprinters	55.7	Bookkeepers	38.6
Auto mechanics	54.6	Nurses	38.4
Assemblers	52.7	Laundry and drycleaning operatives	38.3
Shipping and receiving clerks	50.0	Secretaries	37.3
Draftsmen	34.2	Accountants and auditors	30.8
Accountants and auditors	33.3	Stenographers	28.4
Lawyers	30.3	Technicians, medical and dental	23.6
Aeronautical engineers	26.2	Elementary schoolteachers	19.4
Electrical engineers	20.3	Librarians	16.4

Source: T. Sterling and J. Weinkam, "Smoking Characteristics by Type of Employment," *Journal of Occupational Medicine* 18 (1976): 743–54.

than blue-collar jobs, and blue-collar jobs generally entail a stronger separation between work and consumption than white-collar jobs. Therefore, since white-collar work is generally more interesting and fun than blue-collar work, and to the extent that white-collar workers generally enjoy much more job-related and on-the-job consumption than blue-collar workers, basic economic principles would predict lower rates of absenteeism among white-collar workers than among blue-collar workers. Such a prediction implies, in turn, more absenteeism among smokers than among nonsmokers, but for reasons having nothing to do with smoking. Daniel Taylor (1979), for instance, showed both that rates of absenteeism are lower in white-collar occupations than in blue-collar occupations and that within blue-collar occupations, rates of absenteeism are lower among skilled than among unskilled workers. Furthermore, Holcomb and Meigs (1972) have shown that although cigarette smokers have a higher rate of absenteeism than nonsmokers (5.9 percent versus 4.4 percent), pipe and cigar smokers have the lowest absenteeism rate of all—3.2 percent. Those who seek to infer causation from statistical correlation, if they were judicious and consistent, would have to become advocates of pipes and cigars. But what this observation really shows, of course, is the ever-present danger of treating heterogeneous people as if they were homogeneous. Pipe and cigar smokers are different from cigarette smokers and nonsmokers. With respect to the point of issue here, pipe and cigar smokers are predominantly found in white-collar occupations and professions, where job-related consumption is high, so their lower rate of absenteeism is economically understandable.

It is typically suggested that the greater absenteeism of smokers, when multiplied by their wage rate, will give a measure of the cost of sickness attributed to smoking, in conformity to the lost-earnings approach to the evaluation of illness and death. However, a day spent on sick leave is rarely completely wasted. Even such an activity as lying in bed and watching television is valuable to the sick person, so in principle, the value of such activities should be subtracted from the lost earnings to arrive at a cost of the lost production due to illness. Furthermore, a consistent application of the line of analysis that assigns a cost to lost work would have to conclude that weekends, holidays, and vacations also impose a cost of lost production upon society, for production is as much diminished by these days away from the workplace as it is by sick leave. Furthermore, sick leave may represent time spent fishing, and the value the worker places on a day of fishing may well exceed the lost output particularly in blue-collar occupations. Such cases would actually represent a social benefit rather than a social cost.

Absenteeism by no means implies illness or injury. Rates of absenteeism imply little, if anything, about states of personal health. For instance, the rate of absenteeism in Western European nations is generally about three times as high as that in the United States. And absenteeism in Japan seems to be about half that in the United States. It is implausible that Americans are twice as sickly as Japanese or that Western Europeans are three times as sickly as Americans. It is far more plausible that all are about equally sickly, but they differ in the costs they suffer if they are absent and the rewards they capture if they are not. The lower the cost of absenteeism to workers and the lower the rewards for working, the higher the rate of absenteeism will be—but for reasons having nothing to do with personal health. Both the generally higher tax rates in Western European nations and the far more extensive programs of social welfare there make the higher absenteeism rates economically understandable.

Joint Costs and Improper Cost Attribution

Efforts to attribute a cost of lost production, as well as a cost of medical care, to smoking commonly and wrongly attribute to smoking the entire amount of what is really a joint cost. This problem arises because smokers and nonsmokers are *not identical* in all respects other than smoking. As noted earlier, smokers are overrepresented among blue-collar occupations. They also consume, on average, an above-average amount of alcohol, although there are many teetotaling smokers and nonsmoking alcoholics.[4] Smokers surely exercise less than nonsmokers, although there are smoking bicyclists, swimmers, and joggers.

In assuming that people are identical except for their smoking, various diseases and their associated costs are improperly attributed to smoking. Consider the hypothetical situation illustrated by table 3–5. The population is assumed to be evenly divided between smokers and nonsmokers, with nonsmokers having 100 cases of a disease and smokers having 200 cases. This information is shown in column (3) of table 3–5. If the cost per illness were, say, $1,000, the cost of smoking would be $100,000, according to the common approach—the product of the 100 excess cases of illness attributed to smoking and the cost per disease.

But now consider the additional information conveyed by columns (1) and (2). The interpretation of this information is that nonsmoking nonexercisers and exercising smokers both have twice the illness rate of nonsmoking exercisers, while smoking nonexercisers have four times the illness rate of nonsmoking exercisers. For both smokers and nonsmokers, there are twice as many cases of illness among nonexercisers as among exercisers. A consideration of this example makes it clear that the $100,000 that would be commonly attributed to smoking is wrong, because it would attribute to smoking what could alternatively and equally plausibly be attributed as a cost of failing to exercise.

If smoking were eliminated, illnesses would fall from 300 cases to 200 cases, thus appearing to confirm the standard approach to estimating the cost of smoking. In this case, the 67 illnesses among smoking exercisers would be reduced to 33 illnesses among exercising nonsmokers, and the 133 illnesses among smoking nonexercisers would be reduced to 67 illnesses among nonsmoking nonexercisers. However, table 3–5 can be collapsed by columns as well as by rows. This can be done by converting the nonexercisers into exercisers. The outcome would be the same as before. The 67 illnesses among nonexercising nonsmokers would become 33 ill-

Table 3–5

Smoking, Exercise, and Health: A Hypothetical Illustration

| | Number of Disease Cases | | |
	Exercisers (1)	Nonexercisers (2)	Total (3)
Nonsmokers	33	67	100
Smokers	67	133	200
Total	100	200	300

nesses among nonsmoking exercisers, and the 133 illnesses among smoking nonexercisers would become 67 illnesses among exercising smokers. In this alternative and equally reasonable formulation, the 100 excess cases of illness would be attributed not to smoking but to failing to exercise.

Although the numbers in this example are hypothetical, the point that the example illustrates is real: When health and any associated costs are a joint product of several variables or activities, it is illegitimate to attribute any health consequences to one particular variable or activity. In the case illustrated by table 3–5, smoking could be said to cause 100 cases of illness. But it is equally reasonable to say that smoking causes no diseases and that all diseases can be attributed instead to the failure to exercise. Furthermore, it would be as reasonable to distribute the cases equally between smoking and failing to exercise as it would be to choose *any* particular distribution of cases between the two sources of illness.

If the illustration were made more complex and realistic—such as by adding information about such other characteristics as drinking, weight, occupation, family stress, and so on—the arbitrariness involved in assessing a "cost of smoking" would multiply. Capriciousness or prejudice can easily replace science in such a setting. Someone who does not like smoking can assign the costs to smoking; someone who does not like sedentary life-styles can assign the costs to inactivity; someone who does not like alcohol can assign the costs to drinking; and so on. Any proposition can be supported but, equally and by implication, there is *no* proposition that *must* be supported—that is, there is no unique conclusion that must be drawn from such data.

Who Loses Lost Production— Smokers or Nonsmokers?

The central issue raised by studies of the lost-production costs of smoking (as well as of the medical costs) is simply this: Is smoking a source of harm to Americans in general, or is it simply a source of harm to smokers—if, indeed, it is a source of harm to anyone? Even if we accept the proposition that the lost-production cost of smoking exceeds the direct cost of cigarettes by about $40 billion, an issue of public policy arises only to the extent that those costs are borne by nonsmokers. For if they are borne by smokers, the situation is the same as it is with any act of consumption: people pay for what they buy. In this case, the $40 billion saving that would result from the cessation of smoking would *not* accrue to the residents of the nation in general—giving them an average gain of $200 per person per year—but rather would accrue to the 50 million or so smokers, who would each gain about $800, though at the sacrifice of the benefits they derive from smoking.

It is essential to distinguish between a cost to an individual and a cost to society. For example, suppose that a paper mill discharges wastes into a river, thereby destroying fishing and other recreational uses downstream. The buyers of the mill's products must pay for resources used directly in the mill's production—such as wood, acid, labor, and the like—but not, by assumption, for the damage inflicted on downstream users. The cost to "society" of the mill's operation is the damage imposed on people who are not party to the transactions between the mill and its customers. To speak of a cost to "society," in other words, has meaning only in contrast to a cost to "customers"; a cost to society is a cost that is borne by third parties, not by the parties to a transaction.

It is fallacious to apply principles derived from settings in which diseases are acquired involuntarily because they are inherent in nature to settings in which diseases may be acquired as a by-product of personal choices. In the case of, say, polio or malaria, there is no offsetting beneficial activity for which the disease represents a by-product or possible side effect. But the setting is quite different in such cases as so-called smoking-related diseases or chain saw accidents. In these cases, any costs of usage may be reflected in the demand for the products in the first place, in which case the choice of people to consume the product in question affirms that they value the product more highly than the negative evaluation they place on those costs.

Consider, for example, someone choosing between a chain saw and a hand saw for pruning trees. Chain saws can inflict much more severe bodily harm than hand saws can, but chain saws also save energy and time. The perceived likelihood or cost of an accident is part of the cost of choosing the chain saw. The more dangerous people perceive chain saws to be, the lower their demand for chain saws will be. A buyer's decision to buy a chain saw instead of a hand saw means that the buyer values the chain saw more highly than its cost—the things he must give up to get the saw. That cost includes both the direct cost of the chain saw and the indirect cost of such incidents of ownership as possible accidents.

Why should it be any different for smoking? The cost of smoking includes both the price that people must pay for cigarettes and, in the event that smoking is presumed to damage health, the indirect cost they must bear in terms of diminished health. Someone who chooses to smoke, then, judges that the value he or she derives from smoking exceeds the *sum* of the price of cigarettes and cost of any damaged health that is anticipated to result from smoking. Even if smoking were known to impair health, there would be no cost to society from smoking. Any such cost would be a personal cost borne by smokers, who by their choices have shown that they value smoking more than the sum of the price of cigarettes and any diminished health that results.

Consider, again, the proposition that smokers are absent from work more often than nonsmokers. It might reasonably be expected that a person who misses more work than another will earn less. If people who take an extra three days off per year earn less than those who do not, this loss of earnings would reflect a cost of smoking if the absence was caused by smoking, but this cost would be borne by the smoker. This lost production is reflected in market-determined income payments, and those payments already reflect the value of the lost output. Therefore, to count that lost production as a social cost of smoking is to count the same thing twice.

At first glance, it might appear that although this example might be applicable to a piece-rate system of wage determination, it is less than fully applicable to many contemporary industrial settings. For instance, to the extent that collective bargaining agreements make uniform provisions for sick leave, a higher rate of absenteeism among smokers than among nonsmokers would represent the imposition of a cost on nonsmokers by smokers. As the total amount of absenteeism rises, the average productivity and compensation paid will fall. Other things being the same, firms in which employees average ten absentee days per year will pay more than firms in which the average rate of absenteeism is fifteen days. Hence, if all workers receive the same compensation regardless of the amount of sick leave they take (up to the allowed limit), those who take less leave are made worse off by those who take more leave. If smokers take twelve days of sick leave and nonsmokers take eight days, and if there are an equal number of smokers and nonsmokers, all workers will receive wages as if they had missed ten days. Consequently, nonsmokers will receive two days' less pay than they actually worked, allowing smokers to receive two days' more pay than they actually worked.

However, this situation is not so simple as it might appear. For instance, why were twelve days of sick leave allowed? Why weren't only eight days allowed? Firms that allow only eight days leave will be able to pay higher wages than firms that allow twelve days. But if workers place a higher value on the ability to take off four extra days at their discretion than they place on the higher wages that would otherwise result, they would prefer the employment alternative that offered more sick leave. And people in the opposite position would prefer the other employment option. In either case, sick leave policies are but part of an overall package of compensation, and they tend to reflect employee preferences.

Furthermore, it is necessary to ask why some people would take only eight days off when they were allowed twelve. It might be that they thought that better attendance would improve their prospects for promotion or for a better assignment. Even though those people who missed only eight days of work would receive the same income this year as those who missed twelve days of work, they would expect, on average, to have higher incomes in future years. If so, no questions of social cost arise, because those who are absent more frequently are earning less with respect to expected or lifetime earnings even if not with respect to present earnings. Alternately, people with low rates of absenteeism might not like to stay at home because they dislike being around their spouses or children and because they have no interest in fishing or golfing, whereas people with high rates of absenteeism are in the opposite position. In this case, as in the preceding case, the difference in rates of absenteeism does not reflect some transfer between workers; rather, it reflects differences among workers in their preferences for work, family companionship, and leisure.

What About the Benefits of Smoking?

It is surely peculiar that discussions of smoking have concentrated so intently on the alleged cost of smoking that they have tended to ignore the benefits of smoking almost completely. Yet when we observe people willingly purchasing and using tobacco products, we can infer that the benefits people derive from smoking are, *at a minimum,* equal to the price they pay for cigarettes. To return to the standard illustration used in chapter 2, suppose that the resource cost (tobacco, paper, and so on) of a pack of cigarettes is 80 cents, but the price of cigarettes is $1.20 per pack because taxes are 40 cents per pack. Further suppose that people buy 28 billion packs annually when the price is $1.20. The value of an additional pack of cigarettes is $1.20, but the cost of an additional pack is only 80 cents. In this case, as we explained in chapter 2, the cigarette tax imposes an excess burden, or pure waste, in that it prevents people from exchanging something they value at 80 cents to get something they value at $1.20.

In total, smokers are paying $33.6 billion for cigarettes (28 billion packs at $1.20 per pack). Their benefits from smoking are at least this much, as evidenced by their choice to buy the cigarettes rather than buying something else, and normally exceed this amount. Cigarettes are worth $1.20 per pack to smokers when 28 billion packs are available annually. But if only a lesser amount were available—say, 20 billion packs—smokers will value cigarettes more highly, as evidenced by their willingness to pay more for cigarettes—say, $2.40 per pack. And if only 10 billion packs were available, they might be willing to pay, say, $4.20 per pack. The total value of cigarettes to smokers is the sum of the $33.6 billion and the amount by which the value smokers would place on various amounts less than 28 billion packs exceeds $1.20.

But where do the alleged lost-productivity costs, as well as medical costs, of smoking fit into this type of analysis? Suppose that in addition to the $33.6 billion smokers pay for cigarettes, they bear lost-productivity (or medical) costs of $33.6 billion. Should not this amount be subtracted from any measure of benefits or, equivalently, added to cost? For instance, suppose, in the present illustration, that the total benefits of smoking were $60 billion. This figure would be the sum of (1) the amount people actually pay for cigarettes and (2) the excess of their willingness to pay over what they actually have to pay. Would not the net benefits of smoking be negative in this case? Although the gross benefits are, by postulation, $60 billion, the total costs of smoking are $67.2 billion.

Despite whatever plausibility such an approach might have at first glance, it involves a form of double counting and therefore is erroneous. The double counting arises because such health effects as those regarding lost production are already incorporated into the demand for cigarettes. To the extent that smoking damages health, increases absenteeism, and reduces earnings, the demand for cigarettes will be less than it would otherwise be, in exactly the same way that the demand for chain saws will be lower with higher perceived risks of accidents to buyers. At any given price, people will buy fewer cigarettes, the higher their perception of the health cost. To incorporate lost production as an aspect of the cost of smoking, suppose that smokers are absent four days more per year than nonsmokers, and further suppose that this greater absenteeism is due to smoking. If smokers smoke an average of 400 packs per year, it can be said that each pack is responsible for one-hundredth of a day of absenteeism. If smokers earn $80 per day, this means that each pack of cigarettes cost them, in expected value terms, 80 cents in lost earnings.

The cost of smoking has two components: (1) the price smokers pay, which is $1.20 per pack including tax; and (2) smokers' greater absenteeism and the lost earnings this implies, which is equivalent to 80 cents per pack. Consumers buy 28 billion packs and pay a total price of $2 per pack. But the value of a pack of cigarettes in this case is also $2. The reason for this is that the market demand for cigarettes itself reflects any perceived risks people associate with smoking. This can be seen by asking what would happen to the demand for cigarettes if their negative health effects were to vanish. At a market price of $1.20, people would no longer buy only 28 billion packs; rather, they would buy a larger amount—say, 42 billion packs—just as they would buy more chain saws at the same price if the risks of accidents were to disappear. In short, we can think of a risk-free demand for cigarettes or for chain saws as well as an actual demand, which represents the risk-free demand *discounted by any risks* that smokers or sawers think they have to bear.

What this analysis shows is that the cost of consuming 28 billion packs of cigarettes per year—$56 billion—is also a minimum estimate of the benefit of smoking. In this case, however, smokers pay for cigarettes through two different types of transactions: the $1.20 they pay for each pack they buy and the $80 they lose for each extra day of work they miss. The latter transaction may reveal itself through slower rates of advancement rather than through immediate reductions in earnings, but it will be equivalent to 80 cents per pack in any event. Hence, smokers pay $33.6 billion to vendors for cigarettes, and they forfeit $22.4 billion (28 billion packs at $0.80 per pack) through their absenteeism.

Misinformation, Habituation, and the Demand for Cigarettes

Undergirding our discussion of people's willingness to pay for a product being discounted by the risks they associate with use of that product is an assumption that smokers are reasonably aware of the costs of smoking and that they take these costs into account in choosing whether or not to smoke. However, it is sometimes argued that smokers are poorly informed about the costs of smoking and therefore make choices they later regret. If this were so, the preceding analysis of the effect of lost production on the demand for cigarettes would be inapplicable. In the presence of misinformation, it cannot be claimed that people's willingness to buy cigarettes reflects an appropriate netting out of the health consequences of smoking. An extreme form of misinformation would have smokers totally unaware of possible health effects. In this case, people would buy 28 billion packs per year at a price of $1.20 per pack, thinking, wrongly, that this is all they were paying. If they were aware that they were also paying 80 cents per pack indirectly through lost income, they would buy fewer cigarettes—say, 24 billion packs per year.

The possible presence of misinformation raises, in turn, a question of whether there is any reasonable standard against which it can be judged whether or not people are "reasonably" informed about the health implications of cigarette smoking. Surely, the continued existence of smoking cannot itself serve as evidence that people are insufficiently aware of the health hazards of smoking, because that observed conduct is also consistent with the presumption either that people disagree with the Surgeon General about the existence of those health hazards or that they regard the benefits from smoking as outweighing those potential hazards.

In light of the substantial antismoking campaign of the past two decades or so, the possibility cannot be ruled out that if there is any systematic misinformation on this matter, it errs in the direction of exaggerating the health hazards of smoking. There is surely much more awareness about claims such as those advanced by the Surgeon General and supporting groups than there is about the complex arguments about how statistical correlation implies nothing about physiological causation on the other side of the controversy about smoking and health. If so, it is plausible that people's perceptions of a risk from smoking seem to be more strongly held than would be warranted by the scientific knowledge to date. This is because statistical association is simple to see, but arguments about causation are much more complex and difficult to make and to understand; therefore, people might place more credence in claims that smoking causes disease than those claims logically warrant. In any event, ignorance about the claims of health hazards cannot be adduced as a reason people continue to smoke. The hypothesis that people derive benefits from smoking in excess of the cost—including both the price of cigarettes and the perception of risk—cannot be easily dismissed.

Habituation raises a somewhat different point, but it is used to support the same arguments—namely, that the willingness of people to buy cigarettes does not genuinely reflect the value they place upon cigarettes. There is, of course, a large degree of habituation in all consumption, in the sense that people seek to repeat activities they enjoy. How is being "habituated" to cigarettes any different from being habituated to chewing gum, ice cream, television, jogging, or swimming? Much of what is meant by habituation is simply an efficient representation of someone's preferences. We know that people can change their habits if they truly want to. For instance, heavy eating may be a pleasant habit and vigorous exercise may be distinctly boring, but people can lose weight if they are willing to pay the price. Some people will lose weight; others will not. It surely makes less sense to say that those who do not lose weight are habituated to food while those who do lose weight are not, than to say that some people value losing weight more highly than others, are thus willing to pay a higher price to overcome their eating "habit," and so ultimately are more successful in losing weight.

Cigarettes are sometimes placed in a different category from other "habits" such as overeating, because there are many smokers who claim to want to stop but do not. There are, of course, many overeaters who claim they want to lose weight but do not, but the argument is asserted more strongly for cigarettes. There are many ex-smokers, so we know that people can stop smoking, just as they can stop overeating, if they are willing to pay the price—that is, if they value more highly the benefits they think they will derive from reducing their eating or from stopping their smoking than they value the continuation of their present eating or smoking practices.

But how prevalent is the professed wish among smokers to stop smoking? It is clear that many smokers say that they would like to stop. Atkinson and Townsend (1977) and Leu (1984), for instance, reported survey findings that from 40 to 75 percent of smokers would prefer to quit smoking but are "unable" to do so. And it is equally clear that for most of them, the intensity of that wish is weak, as judged by the observation that they continue to smoke. Should we therefore say that the demand for cigarettes is somehow fraudulent? Perhaps, alternatively, it is the professed desire to stop smoking that is misleading.

In his study of the reasons people give for starting to smoke, Charles Spielberger (1986) found two main themes: (1) adventure and (2) peer emulation. The former is exemplified by such responses as "See if I would enjoy it" and "Try something new," and the latter is exemplified by such responses as "Because most of my friends smoke," "Thought it was satisfying because other people smoke," and "Made me feel more relaxed around my friends." These five responses dominated all other reasons people gave for starting to smoke, as reported by Spielberger.

However, the reasons people gave for *continuing* to smoke, as opposed to starting to smoke, were quite different. They had to do with personally felt benefits that had little in common with the largely externally driven reasons for starting to smoke. The two predominant reasons people gave for continuing to smoke were "Because I enjoy it" and "Relaxes me when I'm upset or nervous." Such externally driven reasons as "Because most of my friends smoke" or "Media advertisements" ranked toward the end of a ten-item list. And even such a response as "Makes me feel more comfortable around my friends" achieved only a middle ranking among the reasons for continuing to smoke.

If peer pressures are strong in the choice to begin smoking, they can also play a role in protestations about both the desire to stop smoking and the "inability" to do so successfully. If most of a person's associates do not smoke, that person will generally sense stronger pressure to stop smoking than will someone who associates mostly with smokers. Each person may derive the same pleasure from smoking and may not really want to quit, but as the percentage of nonsmoking associates rises, the sensed peer pressures to quit smoking will surely rise. In this setting there are two main options. One is the defiant approach: "Regardless of what you say, I like to smoke and I have no intention of quitting." The other is to invoke an excusatory pleading: "I've been trying to quit, but this habit has got the best of me so far. Do you have any suggestions?" Surely, the second approach dominates in human relations in which the "offending" party is in the minority, and it calls into question the reliability of the survey figures that purport to show that many smokers would like to quit smoking but "can't." A plausible alternative explanation is that the protesting smokers really do not want to quit but feel a need to say that they would like to.

Notes

1. In symmetrical fashion, if smokers have a lower hospitalization rate than nonsmokers, their reduced rate of hospitalization would be credited to smoking.
2. We should note that the OTA report was simply a survey of primary research, not primary research itself. Its importance is largely political, in that it represents a continuation of efforts to push an official government position regarding both the effect of smoking on health and the economic consequences of that presumed effect. For a few examples of primary research efforts in this vein, see Doll and Peto (1981), Hammond (1966), and Ravenholt (1984).
3. For strong support for the thesis that smoking has not been shown to impair workplace efficiency, see, for instance, Solmon (1983) and Vogel (1985).
4. Shillington (1977) reported that 92 percent of people classified as alcohol abusers are smokers. (It should perhaps be noted, though, that most smokers are not classified as alcohol abusers.)

4
Smoking and the Cost of Medical Care

E ven though people may miss work because of illnesses or deaths that are attributed to smoking, the cost of any resulting lost production is borne by the smokers, not by the nonsmoking members of society. But can the same be said about the medical expenses that are associated with the treatment of smoking-related illnesses? Those expenses are also substantial. The Office of Technology Assessment report estimated that they were roughly half as much as the cost of lost production—ranging from $12 billion to $35 billion in 1985, with a "best" estimate of $22 billion. This "best" estimate is about 70 cents per pack, which is about twice the present tax burden on cigarettes.

Some of these medical expenses are, of course, financed personally. To the extent that they are, they would seem to be a burden for smokers but not for nonsmokers, and they would be analytically equivalent to the cost of lost production. However, a substantial portion of medical expenses is financed by third parties, either through private insurance programs or through such tax-financed programs as Medicare and Medicaid. Such third-party financing would seem to open the possibility that an increased use of medical resources by smokers involves a shifting of the burden from smokers to nonsmokers. Whether this is actually so— and if it is so, the extent to which it becomes possible to consider that the medical costs associated with smoking represent a social rather than a personal cost—is the primary subject matter of this chapter.

Attribution of Medical Costs to Smoking

The medical expenses attributed to the treatment of so-called smoking-related illnesses are estimated in essentially the same way as the cost of lost production. A figure is derived for the total medical expenses associated with a particular illness, an estimate is made of the share of those expenses attributable to smoking, and a figure for the medical cost of smoking is consequently derived. Although there have been differences in details among particular authors, this general format has informed all such studies.

For instance, suppose that a hospital's annual expenses are $30 million, with which it is able to provide 100,000 patient-days or bed-days of care during a year. This gives an average expense of $300 per bed or per patient. Once this determination of overall cost has been made, the next step is to derive an estimate of the share of hospital usage that reflects the excess demand of smokers. Suppose that someone estimates that the number of bed-days during a year would be 20 percent less if no one smoked. By the standard procedure for attributing cost, $6 million—20 percent of expenses—would be attributed as the hospitalization cost due to smoking.

Essentially the same procedure is used to derive an estimate of the excess physician expenses incurred in the treatment of smoking-related illnesses. Suppose that a physician has 5,000 consultations with patients in one year, and the expense of these consultations is $100,000. If someone estimates that the demand for physicians' services would be 25 percent less if no one smoked, 25 percent of the cost of physician services would be attributed to smoking. This would be $25,000 in the illustration at hand.

In the various studies of smoking and health, it is common to attribute about 85 to 95 percent of the expenses of hospitals and physicians for the treatment of lung cancer to smoking, although there are some substantial variations among authors. And it is common to treat about 15 to 25 percent of the expenses of hospitals and physicians for the treatment of heart disease and chronic bronchitis and emphysema as being due to smoking, though again there are some substantial variations among authors. The exact rates of attribution vary with a number of factors, including the sex and age of the patient. Although various complex considerations can arise in making such attributions, once such an attribution has been made, it becomes a relatively simple computational matter to derive an estimated cost of smoking.

For example, consider Shillington's (1977) estimate of the medical expenses associated with smoking in Canada. He started with data on the number of patient-days spent in hospitals for four diseases: lung cancer, coronary heart disease, bronchitis, and emphysema. He estimated that the average expense of a patient-day in Canada in 1971 was $61.71. By multiplying this daily expense figure by the number of patient-days in each of the four disease categories, Shillington derived estimates of the total hospitalization expenses that could be attributed to each of four categories: $17.9 million for lung cancer, $174.5 million for coronary heart disease, $13.6 million for bronchitis, and $9.3 million for emphysema. To estimate the share of these expenses that can be attributed to smoking, it is necessary to attribute a share of each illness to smoking—that is, to estimate the amount by which the illness would decline if no one smoked.

Shillington developed both a method for attribution based on different age categories and a range of attribution rates for each disease to reflect different underlying assumptions. To simplify a complex procedure, the average attribution rates ranged from 48 to 63 percent for lung cancer, from 6 to 15 percent for coronary heart disease, from 29 to 53 percent for bronchitis, and from 28 to 69 percent for emphysema. Multiplying these rates by the estimated total hospital expenses for each of the four disease categories gives an estimated cost of smoking for each category. These estimated amounts ranged from $8.66 million to $11.2 million for lung cancer, from $10.1 million to $25.9 million for coronary heart disease, from $4.0 million to $7.2 million for bronchitis, and from $2.6 million to $6.4 million for emphysema. In total, the hospitalization cost of smoking in Canada for 1971 was estimated to range from $25.3 million to $50.7 million. When the same estimation procedure was applied to the costs of physicians' services, the estimated range was $2.8 million to $5.4 million.

This procedure is a standard one, and it has been applied in numerous other instances. For instance, Luce and Schweitzer

(1977) estimated that the medical cost of smoking in the United States was $13.4 billion in 1975, which would be about twice as costly in 1986 dollars. Similarly, Egger (1978) estimated that the hospital costs in 1976–77 in Australia were in the $20.6 million to $31.2 million range. He also developed estimates for the costs of physicians' services and prescription drugs attributable to smoking—$4.9 million to $8.2 million and $5.9 million to $11.5 million, respectively.

There are plausible grounds for thinking that this common procedure overstates the medical costs of smoking. (We should perhaps restate here that we are speaking of *assumed*, not proved, *causal* relationships when we speak of the medical costs of smoking.) A primary reason for this bias is that although lung cancer is a relatively inexpensive form of cancer to treat, the standard approach to estimating medical expenses assumes that lung cancer uses the same medical resources as other forms of cancer. The attribution of 30 percent of cancer deaths to smoking does not warrant the attribution of 30 percent of the estimated medical costs of treating all cancers to smoking. The proper attribution rate would be considerably lower. Most lung cancer deaths occur relatively quickly after diagnosis and do not involve elaborate, long-term methods of treatment. Just how much of a bias results from such "average cost" pricing we do not know, but we do know that attributing to smoking a share of the medical expenses equal to the rate at which particular diseases are attributed to smoking overstates the medical costs of smoking.

Medical Costs, Personal Responsibility, and Insurance

To the extent that people pay their own medical expenses, any medical expenses that are due to the treatment of smoking-related illnesses would be paid by smokers and would not be a burden on nonsmokers. The analysis of medical expenses in such a regime of personal responsibility would be essentially the same as the analysis of lost production we examined in chapter 3. Any such medical expenses would be part of the cost of smoking to smokers, and the higher those costs are, the lower will be the net demand for cigarettes. In other words, the market demand for cigarettes would reflect a discount for the medical expenses people associate with smoking. Medical expenses would be personal, not social, costs. Therefore, data such as those presented in the Office of Technology Assessment report, which portray smoking-related medical costs in the range of $12 billion to $35 billion, would represent costs that are largely borne by smokers, not by nonsmokers.

Although people do pay some of their medical expenses directly out of their own pockets, many of those expenses are covered by various insurance programs. Moreover, over the postwar period, personal payments have become of ever-diminishing importance in the financing of medical care. Third-party payments—payments made either by governments or by insurance companies, not by individuals—now comprise about 90 percent of hospital expenses and over 50 percent of physician's expenses. Third-party payments create a network of transfers among people, and those transfers open the possibility that smokers impose costs on nonsmokers. An increase in the medical expenses that smokers incur will increase insurance premiums for the nonsmoking members of an insurance program and will increase taxes for nonsmoking taxpayers in the case of government-financed medical care. In either case, an increase in medical costs incurred by smokers will be paid in part by nonsmokers. So long as the provision of medical care is financed, at least in part, through insurance or taxation, those who make relatively high use of medical resources will place added financial burdens upon those who make relatively low use.

In comparing personal responsibility with insurance as forms of paying for medical care, it is important to distinguish between ex ante (before the fact) and ex post (after the fact) perspectives. When insurance payments are looked at after the fact, people who are sick more often seem to be subsidized by those who are not. But this is true of all insurance programs when they are viewed after the fact. People who have automobile accidents seem to be subsidized by those who do not. People whose homes are damaged or destroyed by fire seem to be subsidized by those whose homes are not. People who require medical care seem to be subsidized by people who do not. All insurance has the ex post property of appearing to subsidize some people at the expense of others.

But the appropriate perspective toward insurance is ex ante. From this ex ante perspective, all participants must look upon their participation as beneficial; otherwise, they would not have chosen to participate in the first place. People choose to participate in an insurance program because they judge that the benefits of coverage in the event of accident or illness are worth the price of participation, even though the most likely outcome is that their total premium payments will exceed their total claims.

To say this is not to claim that insurance programs work perfectly in attributing risk to different categories of buyers. Attribution may be imperfect, and to the extent that it is, some buyers will be subsidized at the expense of others. In many cases, government regulation of insurance is a source of such subsidization by preventing the refinement of risk categories. This is illustrated, for instance, by automobile insurance regulation, which, by restricting the refinement of risk categories, had the effect of requiring low-risk categories of drivers to subsidize high-risk categories. Insurance is also subject to moral hazard, in that the availability of insurance reduces care on the part of insured parties and so increases accidents and claims. For this reason, medical expenses are likely to be higher under insurance finance than under personal finance, even if people fall into the same risk category. Moreover, insurance can also encounter problems of adverse selection, which can arise because people who are particularly likely to have claims will have particularly strong demands for insurance coverage. If the information about personal characteristics that govern probable claims is available to buyers but not insurance companies, claims for payment, and base premiums, will rise.

What About Government-Subsidized Medical Care?

The situation might seem different for government-provided subsidies for medical care. A commonly expressed sentiment is that everyone has an interest in smoking because such programs as

Medicaid and Medicare cover a significant portion of the medical bills for smokers. This sentiment was illustrated by the claim in the 11 May 1982 issue of the *Wall Street Journal* that "Uncle Sam has a budgetary interest in the cigarette toll [on health] because Medicaid and Medicare pick up a significant part of the medical bills for afflicted smokers." If smoking damages health, increased claims under Medicare and Medicaid seem a distinct possibility. Indeed, this possible positive relationship between smoking and resulting claims under Medicare and Medicaid has been used to advocate earmarking of tobacco tax revenues for the support of Medicare.

However, this case for earmarking is questionable on both factual and analytical grounds. Factually, even if it is assumed that smoking harms health, there is no basis for claiming that smokers place an above-average demand on Medicare. It is incorrect simply to compare two sets of people at the same age, to note that the smokers have higher medical bills than the nonsmokers, and subsequently to conclude that smokers consume an above-average amount of medical resources.

One facet of any smoking-induced health impairment is that smokers have shorter life spans. For instance, Cowell and Hirst (1980) concluded that smokers have a life expectancy 7.3 years less than that of nonsmokers. Such a finding is certainly consistent with charging smokers higher premiums than nonsmokers for the same life insurance coverage. However, it is also consistent with charging them *less* for lifetime health insurance—and Medicaid/Medicare is a form of open-ended, lifetime health insurance. With shorter life spans, smokers make less use of extended stays in hospitals and convalescent homes where the expenses can become particularly heavy, in the later years of life, when many of the expenses are covered by Medicare and Medicaid. A smoker who dies seven years before his nonsmoking neighbor will not be around to make those especially costly claims that occur later in life.

The correct question regarding subsidization under Medicare and Medicaid does not involve a comparison between smokers and nonsmokers at the same age; it involves a comparison between smokers and nonsmokers with respect to the present value of their lifetime medical expenses. In this regard, Leu and Schaub (1983) developed a simulation model for Switzerland under the assumption that no one smoked after 1876.[1] They sought, among other things, to compare actual medical expenses in Switzerland in 1976 with what they projected those expenses would have been if no one had smoked after 1876. Underlying their work was the presumption that smoking damages health. Therefore, the cessation of smoking in 1876 would have led to a larger and older population in 1976 than the population that actually existed in Switzerland. However, Leu and Schaub estimated that medical expenses would have been roughly the same as they actually were in 1976. In other words, the negative health effect of smoking does not imply that smokers impose costs on nonsmokers, even when health care is provided in part by government.

But suppose smokers, over their lifetime in present value terms, do make greater use than nonsmokers of medical resources subsidized by government. There is still an analytical question concerning whether this raises an issue of external cost or whether it raises only an issue of income transfer. There seems little doubt that the growth of third-party medical payments has contributed to the relative shift of resources into the provision of medical care, as is illustrated by table 4–1. In 1960, health care took up 5.1 percent of the Gross National Product, up less than one percentage point from 1950. And in 1965, health care took up 5.6 percent of the GNP. It was

Table 4–1

Medical Care Spending as a Share of the Gross National Product

Year	Medical Care Spending (billions)	Percentage of GNP
1950	$ 12.0	4.2
1960	25.9	5.1
1965	38.9	5.6
1970	69.2	7.0
1975	124.7	8.0
1980	237.8	9.0
1982	347.1	10.5

Source: Ann Kollman Bixby, "Social Welfare Expenditures, 1963–83," *Social Security Bulletin* 49(February 1986), table 7.

then that Medicare and Medicaid began, and with them the start of significant amounts of tax-financed medical care. Within a decade, medical care's share of the GNP had increased to 8 percent, and since then it increased at a similar rate.

People will clearly consume more of anything, medical care included, when that consumption is subsidized than when it is not. In economics, however, the distinction between a transfer and a social cost is a fundamental one: the former refers to a redistribution of total income, whereas the latter refers to a reduction in total income, although, of course, the two may well occur together. Subsidized medical care is clearly a program that transfers income from people who make below-average claims to people who make above-average claims. With respect to smoking, an external cost will arise from subsidized medical care only to the extent that it induces people to smoke more, with that increased smoking leading, in turn, to greater illness and higher medical expenses.

The existence of subsidized medical care surely gives, at most, a faint incentive for people to become more sickly. Hence, removal of subsidized medical care would have little if any effect on the amount of smoking and, thereby, on the amount of smoking-induced disease. Removing the subsidization of medical care would, of course, reduce the claims people make upon medical resources, but this is a quite different matter. Someone may choose to have a silver dental filling if he has to pay the full cost but a gold filling if two-thirds of the cost is reimbursed under a dental insurance plan. The insurance plan does not induce people to have more cavities, but it does induce them to be more lavish in securing treatment for the cavities they do have. Similarly, smokers, as well as everyone else, will make more use of medical care when it is subsidized than when it is not. The subsidization of anything increases the amount of it that people will use. Medicare and Medicaid encourage people to make greater use of medical resources, but this does not mean that they encourage people to become more sickly than they would otherwise have been. Smoking would seem to have little if any external cost, even if medical expenses are subsidized. Smokers' increased use of medical resources is identical to others' increased use of medical resources, and it is an inevitable outcome of any program of subsidization.

Transfers and Social Costs: A Further Consideration

It is worthwhile to explore more fully why it is that even if smokers do place greater demands on the health care system than other people, it does not follow that they are a source of social cost. Suppose that a smoker on a crowded train platform accidentally burns a hole in the coat of a lady standing next to him. Repairing the damage costs her $50. This is clearly an uncompensated cost. The benefit of smoking accrued to the smoker, whereas the cost of the burned coat was paid by the lady. Alternatively, suppose that a young motorcyclist suffers an accident. He dies of head injuries because he was not wearing a safety helmet, and his widow collects pension payments. The young man enjoyed the benefits of motor-cycling, but through his failure to wear a helmet, he created a situation in which everyone must now contribute through taxation to his widow's pension. Does the payment of the widow's pension also represent a social cost?

The source of the lady's $50 loss was clearly the careless smoker standing beside her. But the source of the loss that taxpayers suffer as their share of the widow's pension was surely not the motorcy-clist, any more than the tobacco farmer was the source of the lady's damaged coat. The source of the higher extractions from taxpayers is the legislature, because the income transfer was created by the state when the legislature decided to provide pensions for widows. Thus, the payment from taxpayers to the widow is a product of state policy.

If we try to go beyond this and specify that some types of transfers constitute social costs while other do not, absurdities quickly arise, with no reasonable or logical basis for including some as social costs and excluding others. The widow of a heavy drinker, a fat man, a football player, or a mine worker must also, by the same criteria, create a social cost. Also perhaps vulnerable to the charge of creating a social cost are people who work too hard, people who do not get the right vitamins, people who do not exercise adequately, and so on. We do not intend to suggest causal relationships here, only to acknowledge the types of conceptual issues that can easily arise in this area. Such considerations also bring into question whether the objective of the policy is to relieve the plight of widows or to reward the widows of men who "lived right." In any event, it is the state, not the injured or deceased, that creates the income transfer, and with it the imposition of any possible loss on other taxpayers. Life is rife with "social costs," which in many cases seem to be created by the very existence of society.

The point of contention about transfers reduces to the issue of the right of access to state-provided benefits and the conditions placed upon that access. Although people have supported or opposed transfer programs on various grounds, we would only note that the mere presence of a transfer payment or system of payments does not legitimize a claim that the recipients of transfers are creating social costs. There may well be social costs in such situations, but making a judgment to this effect involves more than merely observing the existence of a network of transfers from some people to others.

A social cost in the presence of transfers exists only to the extent that such transfers induce changes in personal conduct. Indeed, such changes in personal conduct are an important reason for seeking to foreclose uncompensated costs. Imagine for a moment that every smoker who burned a hole in someone's coat had to pay for the damage. This would remove the uncompensated cost, but more important, it would provide a strong incentive to smokers to be careful with their cigarettes. If smokers were liable for such damages, the annual extent of damage to coats would be reduced. The social gain thus resides in the reduced damage to coats, not in the payments per se to ladies with burned coats. If the necessity to make such payments did not induce smokers to be more careful— with that increased care thereby reducing the extent of burned coats—there would be no social gain from such payments. The payments would merely represent a reversal of the direction of transfer: smokers would become poorer and ladies wearing coats would be richer, but the extent of cigarette-inflicted damage to coats would be unchanged. In this vein, it is surely doubtful whether the repeal of widow's pensions would change the conduct of motorcyclists in a way that would reduce the extent of accidents, whereas it is quite likely that the imposition of damage penalties upon smokers who burn other people's coats will lead smokers to be more careful with their cigarettes.

A transfer can create a problem of social cost only if people change their conduct in response to the presence of the transfer. For instance, if the personal cost of absenteeism were somehow to be eliminated (which may actually be quite difficult to do because of the ability of absenteeism to be reflected in future earnings), the rate of absenteeism would rise because of the lessened personal cost of absenteeism. The resulting reduction in output would be paid for not by those who were absent but by society generally. By insulating a person's decision to be absent from the consequences or costs of that decision, the transfer would create a problem of social, as distinct from personal, cost. This situation is quite unlike the personal reduction in earning that is suffered as a result of injury or illness.

With respect to engaging in such activities as smoking, whether or not the presence of a transfer system for financing medical expenses creates a social cost is ultimately an empirical matter. A social cost will result to the extent that the injection of subsidies into the provision of medical care encourages people to do things that *increase* illness and death. If subsidized medical care leads people to smoke more, resulting in an increased incidence of illness and death, then the transfer program does create a social cost. However, this cost results from the increased mortality and morbidity resulting from the subsidy-induced increase in the amount of smoking; it does not reside in the medical payments per se.

There is no question that people will make greater use of medical resources if that usage is subsidized. But the mere fact of subsidization raises no issue of social cost, for it represents only a transfer from those who make relatively little use of such resources to those who make relatively large use. A social cost will result from the existence of a system of subsidized medical care only to the extent that people do things that make them sicker. Although this outcome is conceivable, it is a remote possibility, and the magnitudes involved would surely be small. What seems to have happened in discussions of the social cost aspects of such transfer programs as subsidized medical care is that people have addressed the wrong question—whether subsidized medical care will induce people to make greater use of medical resources—instead of the right question—whether subsidized medical care will induce more smoking, which, in turn, may lead to more illness and a need for more medical care. Whereas the wrong question can easily and strongly be answered affirmatively, the right question cannot.

Equity considerations have also been injected into discussions of the subsidization of some peoples' medical expenses by others, often under the claim that the tax-transfer system that subsidizes medical expenses provides an unfair subsidy to smokers. This argument about unfairness is worthy of further consideration. The problem with the argument is that there is no clear way to draw the line between smoking, which is seen as a form of voluntary risk, and such activities as skiing, eating too much, swimming, driving, living in urban areas where the air is polluted, and sundry other activities that may also influence health and longevity. All of these activities are self-inflicted in the same sense that smoking is. To try to draw distinctions among these various possibilities is arbitrary; moreover, any effort to draw such distinctions would involve placing before the public agenda the regulation of numerous facets of personal life.

Furthermore, it is inappropriate to look at only one incident of income transfer to determine whether a *net* cost or transfer exists. Everyone in a society stands in some loss or gain status with respect to particular transfer programs. A large number of income transfers take place, and each person is a winner in some and a loser in others. The motorcyclist was a "winner" with respect to widow's pensions, for his wife will draw more from the pension program than he paid in taxes. But as a consumer of sugar, he was a "loser" to the subsidized sugar grower. As a full-time employee, he "lost" on his unemployment insurance. Not being a war veteran, he "lost" on veterans' benefits. And because he died at a young age, he will never get to collect his own retirement benefits under Social Security. In order to know whether, overall, income was transferred *to* him or *from* him, one would have to examine his entire life span, measuring all the intentional and unintentional income transfers in which he was involved.

Income transfers are a ubiquitous product of our political system; indeed, it is possible to explain a wide variety of political outcomes and practices under the assumption that wealth transfers are their only product.[2] The end effect of any one person's life-style may ultimately leave him a "benefactor" of others or a "debtor" to others, in the sense that either more or less was taken from him in taxes than he received through various transfer programs. It is this, above all else, that makes it impossible to say that any particular income transfer constitutes an unfair and uncompensated cost. Any particular program represents only one of many such transactions the individual has within an entire network of tax-transfer relationships that characterize a political order.

Cigarettes, Medicare, and Earmarked Taxation

As noted briefly in chapter 2, there has been considerable interest in recent years in the possibility of earmarking at least part of the cigarette excise tax for the support of Medicare. This interest in earmarking rests upon the belief that smokers impose costs on nonsmokers in that smoking damages health and this impairment, in turn, imposes costs on the remainder of the American citizenry in such forms as higher taxes for Medicare. However, even if we assume for purposes of discussion that smoking harms health, it does not follow that this harmed health imposes costs on nonsmokers—costs that represent the supply of particular medical services to smokers, which, in turn, could indirectly be charged to users through the cigarette excise tax.

User charging is generally considered superior on both equity and efficiency grounds to general-fund financing in cases where user charging is a feasible option.[3] Equity is better served with user charging because the amounts that people pay to support a service vary with how much of the service they use. A person who mails twice as many letters as someone else pays twice as much when postal services are financed by user charges. But if postal services were financed from general revenues, the amounts that different people pay to support postal services would depend not on their use of the mails but on their share of the total tax burden. Two people with the same taxable income would pay the same amount to support postal services, regardless of how many letters they mail. The light user of postal services would pay a greater amount per letter than the heavy user; thus, general-fund financing would subsidize the heavy user at the expense of the light user.

Efficiency is also better served with user charges, because user charges generate information about the value people place on what is being provided. The main question in the provision of any service is whether that service is worth to users what it cost them in their capacities as customers or taxpayers. The prices people pay indicate how highly they value a service. If the sum of those valuations is insufficient to cover cost, information is generated to the effect that users value that service less highly than what it costs. Alternatively, if the amount people are willing to pay exceeds the cost of providing that service, information is generated to the effect that an expansion of output may be desirable. But with general-fund financing, no such information is created about the value people place on different public services. With less information available, efficiency is diminished. User pricing, then, is a method of financing government that can enhance both the equity and the efficiency with which public services are provided.

Tax earmarking occupies an intermediate position between user pricing and general-fund financing. It is a method of indirectly pricing services that would be difficult or impossible to price directly. The general technique of tax earmarking is to tax something that is used in conjunction with the service that cannot be priced directly and to earmark the proceeds of that tax for expenditure upon that service.[4] The primary example of tax earmarking in the United States is the earmarking of gasoline tax revenues for expenditures on highways. The services provided by highways are difficult to price directly, yet the use of highways is essentially no different from the use of telephones. A telephone is used to transport a person's voice from one place to another; a highway is used to transport his car from one place to another. The only difference between highways and telephones is the pragmatic one that it is relatively easy to charge people for their phone calls and relatively difficult to charge them for their use of highways.

Although direct user pricing may not be feasible, an indirect form of user pricing through tax earmarking can serve as a reasonably close substitute under some conditions. If the gasoline tax is 20 cents per gallon, a car that gets twenty miles per gallon is paying, indirectly, a user fee of 1 cent per mile for highways. The central test of tax earmarking is whether it is possible to envision a contractual relationship that would have terms generally corresponding to the terms generated by the earmarked tax. The use of a 20 cents per gallon gasoline tax as an indirect way of charging people 1 cent per mile for their use of highways surely seems, at least as a first approximation, to be in reasonable conformity with the contractual test.

This contractual test is not free from ambiguity, of course, because it requires that the person undertaking the test envision or conjecture the types of agreements people would have made if direct pricing had been possible. Nonetheless, it is possible to distinguish reasonable from unreasonable possibilities. The taxation of gasoline may not operate identically to the direct pricing of highway services, but it surely creates some substantial nexus between the amounts people pay and the services they receive in return. By contrast, the use of a gasoline tax to finance Medicare would be inconceivable as an outcome of some contractual agreement.

The use of gasoline tax revenues to finance mass transit illustrates the irreducible ambiguity that characterizes this contractual test. This use of revenues would not necessarily fail the contractual test. The provision of mass transit might reduce highway congestion, thereby increasing the quality of highway services received by those who continue to drive and to pay the gasoline tax. Even though the diversion of revenues from highways to mass transit might increase the implicit price per mile to, say, 1.25 cents, the resulting reduction in congestion might result in a higher quality of highway service that is worth the higher price, though this need not be so.

Although it is possible to develop principles of tax earmarking as a substitute for user charging, it does not follow that any particular use of tax earmarking necessarily serves, or serves very effectively, in such a capacity. The practice of earmarking may diverge, to a lesser or a greater extent in particular cases, from the principle of earmarking. The closeness of practice to principle may sometimes be difficult to determine, as the example of earmarking gasoline taxes for mass transit illustrates. A point of departure in any effort to reach such a determination is to ask whether the pattern of charges that results from the earmarked tax seems to correspond in general outline to the pattern that would result from the direct charging of users in a contractual setting.

How does the earmarking of tobacco tax revenues for Medicare conform to the principles of tax earmarking? The case for earmarking rests upon two main presumptions. One is that smoking causes an increase in the use of medical resources by people aged sixty-five and over. The other is that, in light of the first presumption, tax earmarking can reasonably be thought to pass the contractual test in a context where direct pricing is infeasible.

The prices people pay for insurance coverage do vary, of course, with the various risk categories into which they are placed. An earmarked cigarette tax might seem to be a way of charging a higher insurance premium to people who occupy a higher risk category. However, just because smokers are presumed to belong to a higher risk category does not mean that they make particularly heavy use of Medicare. As we noted earlier, if smokers do indeed belong to a higher risk category, they may actually make less use of a program such as Medicare. If smoking truly does harm health, the shortened life spans that result mean that smokers make less use of extended stays in hospitals and convalescent homes in the later years of life, when the burdens on Medicare become especially heavy. This possibility is generally consistent with the work of Leu and Schaub (1983) noted earlier.

But suppose, to carry the argument one step further, that we find that smokers do, indeed, have greater medical expenses than nonsmokers over their lifetimes in present value terms. Even in this case—a case about which there presently are no convincing data—it does not follow that the earmarking of the cigarette excise tax to support Medicare is a reasonable way of charging smokers for the medical costs associated with their smoking. This line of argument might have validity if Medicare were truly an insurance program. But if Medicare were truly an insurance program, people would pay directly for their anticipated use of medical resources through their premiums, and the coverage people would receive would depend on the premiums they paid. In this case, however, there would be no need for such an indirect method of pricing as tax earmarking in the first place.

Like all of the Social Security programs, Medicare is not truly an insurance program; its operation does not reflect any effort to apply a commercial principle to government. Medicare is fundamentally a program of subsidized medical care for people over age sixty-five; as such, it is more a transfer or welfare program than an insurance program, with the directions of transfer primarily from younger to older people and from relatively healthy to relatively unhealthy people. This characteristic of Medicare, which is by now widely recognized in the scholarly community if not among the public at large, invalidates the argument that earmarking the tobacco tax for Medicare is a reasonable substitute for user pricing, for the commercial principle is not applicable to Medicare.

Consider two of the several ways in which Medicare is run as a welfare program, not as an insurance program. First, even if current tax payments are looked upon as paying for future medical payments, which is most certainly not the case, people who pay different amounts during their lifetimes would receive correspondingly differing degrees of protection after age sixty-five. People who made larger payments would have bought proportionately more protection. This greater protection might result in longer coverage, a lower coinsurance rate, or any number of numerous other possibilities. But the essential point is that the protection received would vary directly with the payments made under an insurance program. With Medicare, however, the protection received is the same, regardless of the payments made.

Second, if Medicare were truly an insurance program to take effect upon reaching age sixty-five, people would pay funds during their working years that subsequently would be sufficient, with accumulated interest, to pay their hospitalization expenses during their years of retirement. Concomitantly, the payments made under Medicare to any particular age cohort would be limited to the payments plus accumulated interest that that cohort had previously made into Medicare. But when Medicare was instituted in 1965, people immediately began to receive payment of hospitalization expenses, even though they had paid nothing into the program. Medicare in no way embodies contractual principles. Moreover, direct user pricing is surely feasible for Medicare, so there is no case for arguing that tax earmarking is necessary as an indirect form of user charging. Medicare is fundamentally a welfare program—a program that transfers income from some people to others—not a genuine, contractually based program of medical insurance.

One could, of course, advocate the extension of the commercial principle to Medicare, but this would entail a drastically different program from what now exists. So long as the commercial principle is not invoked, and so long as Medicare remains essentially a transfer program, there is no principled basis for saying that one particular subset of users should be subject to commercial or actuarial principles while other subsets are not. There does seem to be a widespread public sentiment that people *do* pay into genuine insurance programs with the various Social Security programs. This sentiment is reinforced by the use of language that speaks of "contributions" rather than of "taxes." If the Social Security programs should come to be seen as welfare programs of taxing and transferring income—with distributions of winners and losers that seem arbitrary and capricious when compared against the standards commonly thought applicable to welfare programs—the support for those programs might weaken. By helping to dispel the illusion of insurance and replacing it with the reality of welfare, general-fund financing might undermine public support for those programs.

Principle, Expediency, and Wealth Transfers

The claim that smokers impose above-average burdens upon health-care programs would be an argument for charging smokers differentially heavier prices for participation in those programs—if the programs were operated along commercial principles. But clearly, they are *not* designed to operate along commercial principles. Such programs embody various patterns of cross-subsidization or wealth transfers. As with insurance programs, people who incur greater

medical expenses than their tax payments to finance the program
are subsidized by people in the reverse position. However, except to
the extent that insurance programs are constrained by state regulation to create patterns of cross-subsidization, any such ex post
cross-subsidization would be unknowable ex ante. Considerations
of transaction costs aside, cross-subsidization at an ex ante level
must be a matter of political power, with the legislature choosing to
subsidize particular sets of people at the expense of others. There
are numerous ways in which this happens, with respect to both the
financing of medical care and the financing of most other governmental programs.

What is the merit of a professed desire to implement user-type
pricing in a particular case, such as by imposing a particularly
heavy tax on smokers to support Medicare or even simply to
support the general fund, as the cigarette tax now does? Such an
effort could, of course, be but one piece of a general program to
operate government more along commercial principles. The total
program might contain many pieces, including replacement of the
retirement insurance component of Social Security by a system of
individual retirement accounts, elimination of all agricultural price
support and crop restriction programs, and privatization of
education, to mention but a few of many possible illustrations.
Such an approach would represent a principled effort to expand
the scope of the application of contractual principles throughout
government.

However, the application of such a contractual approach to
only one service, as in the case of smoking, hardly represents the
application of principle to politics. Rather, it represents expediency
backed by power. In light of the minority position of smokers in
American society—to say nothing of the predominantly blue-collar
status of smokers, which carries relatively low political influence—
the imposition of high and growing tax burdens is not surprising; it
is an understandable reflection of human nature. But rather than
saying that smokers should pay higher taxes because they make
more use of medical resources than others (which is not a demon-
strated proposition in any event), it would be more honest to say
that smokers should pay higher taxes because that would lower the
taxes the rest of us have to pay.

Notes

1. Related findings for Canada are developed in Stoddart et al. (1986).
2. See, for example, McCormick and Tollison (1981).
3. For a survey of issues and literature concerning user charges, see Wagner (1983), pp. 151–70).
4. Aspects of the theory of tax earmarking are presented in Buchanan (1963) and McMahon and Sprenkle (1970).

5

Nonsmokers, External Costs, and State Regulation

I f the opposition to smoking were based exclusively on the alleged adverse health effects to smokers themselves, it would be easy to counter this opposition by simply noting that paternalism is inconsistent with the principles of individual liberty upon which our free, democratic society is based. Simply stated, if individuals choose to smoke despite the probability of adverse health effects, that is their right, and they harm no one but themselves in doing so. The choices of individuals concerning the relative riskiness of their personal behavior is their business, and theirs alone, so long as those choices do not infringe on the rights of others. Few of even the most ardent opponents of tobacco should disagree with this proposition.[1] As we discussed in chapters 3 and 4, whatever costs of lost productivity and medical care result from smoking-induced damage to the health of smokers are borne by the smokers themselves.

In recent years, a new line of argument has emerged in support of restrictions on tobacco. This line of argument acknowledges that smokers are free to damage themselves, but it suggests that smokers also damage the health of nonsmokers who happen to come into contact with tobacco smoke against their will. The claim here is that smokers generate a form of indoor pollution termed *environmental tobacco smoke* (ETS) and that they consequently expose nonsmokers in their vicinity to many of the same adverse health effects they themselves can expect to face.

On its surface, this argument seems the opposite of the paternalistic claim that the government should restrict smoking in order to protect smokers from themselves. There is no direct expression of interest that government act as a busybody or a nanny to protect smokers from themselves. Rather, it is affirmed that government should act as a defender of the rights and liberties of individuals—a governmental role traditionally advocated by even the most ardent proponents of limited governments and free markets. But with respect to smoking, this requires that government protect nonsmokers from the harm that smokers would inflict on them. Restrictions on smoking are thus analogous not to laws preventing free speech or other peaceable behavior but to laws against assault and theft.

It is not our purpose here to comment on or criticize the claim that there is a link between exposure to ETS and various adverse effects on the health of nonsmokers. Although we note that the recent exhaustive survey of the existing scientific research into the effects of ETS exposure by the National Research Council has found that the evidence for adverse health effects is mostly ambiguous and inconclusive—and that where a link may exist, it is based on persistent exposure for a long period of time—we will assume throughout this chapter that there is unambiguous evidence for significant adverse effects of prolonged exposure of nonsmokers to ETS. Our interest here is with the economics of the behavior of individuals with respect to ETS, rather than with any direct medical consequences.[2]

At the outset, it is important to note that the argument about ETS is *not* an argument about whether or not some nonsmokers dislike tobacco. Obviously, some nonsmokers find tobacco smoke annoying. But by the same token, some non–sports fans find sports annoying, some nonvegetarians find vegetables annoying, and so on. Freedom of choice implies freedom to do things that others may dislike. The proper focus of the argument over ETS is simple: Who bears the costs? Economically speaking, it is irrelevant whether or not ETS causes health problems. What is relevant is whether or not smokers impose involuntary costs (either health-related or not) on others.

In this chapter, we shall first examine the economics of restrictions on smoking that are ostensibly designed to prevent the generation of external costs by smokers. We will then consider the problem of environmental tobacco smoke from the perspective of the Coase theorem,[3] considering the extent to which ETS represents the imposition by smokers of uncompensated costs on nonsmokers and subsequently extending this analysis to the problem of children and ETS. Finally, we will assess the relationship between tobacco regulation and the concept of "public health."

The Economics of Clean Indoor Air Acts

Regulations designed to restrict the public consumption of tobacco, which are grounded on the assumption that ETS exposure clearly harms nonsmokers, have been legion in recent years. These forms of legislation are usually referred to as clean indoor air acts, after a 1979 Connecticut bill by that name. The recently passed Proposition P in San Francisco (technically, the Smoking Pollution Control Ordinance), which has received tremendous media attention, is another example. These acts range greatly in severity—Connecticut's 1979 law was very limited in the range of places covered, whereas San Francisco's law is likely to result in the prohibition of smoking in many workplaces—but all have the same basic idea: Smokers must be restricted, by force of law, from imposing their tobacco smoke on unwilling nonsmokers.[4]

As the recent report of the National Research Council (1986) makes clear, there are many unresolved questions regarding the issue of ETS and human disease. By contrast, the costs that will result from the enactment of a clean indoor air act are clear and high. These costs can be broken down into three major categories: the costs to businesses, the costs to the enacting government, and the costs to individuals affected by the law.

The costs to businesses can be usefully broken down further into two major groups: those affecting eating and drinking establishments and those affecting private workplaces, though there are important costs that are common to both. Restaurants can expect to face a significant loss in revenue to fast-food and grocery stores, the exact extent and nature of which will depend on the precise nature of a particular clean indoor air act. Suppose that it is a relatively lax ordinance, requiring merely that a restaurant permitting smoking must provide a separate "smokers only" area. Because the customer mix of smokers and nonsmokers on a given day cannot be known in advance, the owner of such a restaurant would be unable to establish a smoking section of a size that was always optimal. Sometimes he would designate too much space for his nonsmoking section; at other times he would designate too little space (and the same with his smoking section). Consequently, he would frequently have to turn away otherwise willing customers because of the artificial scarcity of table space imposed by the law. With more stringent ordinances like the San Francisco statute, which essentially grant nonsmokers the power to veto *all* smoking on the premises if they so desire, the individual revenue loss is likely to be more straightforward and probably larger. Some smokers will simply choose to stay home or take out food. Other smokers will "vote with their feet" when the restriction applies only to a limited area and will drive into another jurisdiction to buy their meal. Either way, restaurants can be expected to lose significant amounts of revenue, and this revenue loss, in turn, will represent the imposition of a loss on consumers, who will have to spend time finding an alternative restaurant or who will choose to eat out less frequently because eating out has become more costly.[5]

Another cost restaurant owners can be expected to bear is the cost of physically altering their establishments to make them comply with a clean indoor air act where that act requires that nonsmoking areas to be set aside be of a certain size in relation to the building capacity. For example, in a study of the Clean Indoor Air Act in Montgomery County, Maryland, Hamilton and Associates (1982) found that about three-quarters of restaurant-owning respondents judged that the law would require that they make physical alterations to their property, and 16 percent estimated that the alteration would amount to more than $1,000. Also, the signs some laws require add another small—though in some cases significant—cost to complying with the law.

The most important costs likely to result from a clean indoor air act in the private workplace involve productivity losses resulting from compliance. Again, the actual losses will vary from law to law, but they can be quite substantial. Consider the San Francisco ordinance, which requires that employers provide segregated facilities where smokers can smoke and effectively requires that businesses also provide "smoking breaks" for smoking employees, rather than simply allowing them to smoke while working. The cost of the physical arrangements, together with the time lost to production because of smoking breaks that would be necessary for maintaining the morale of smoking employees, may in some cases prove significant.

But there is another cost to the firm that is likely to be more difficult to measure but could have more important and more detrimental consequences. This is the resentment and hostility between smokers and nonsmokers that may result from the imposition of a kind of "tobacco apartheid" in the workplace. If nonsmokers have the legal right to restrict the smoking of their tobacco-smoking fellow workers, resentment between the two groups will represent a potential problem and could adversely affect morale within the company. This lower morale could be difficult to improve and could itself result in a decline in productivity. Many firms are engaged in some kind of team production, and the loss of the team spirit among employees could have serious consequences in terms of firm output.

Finally, clean indoor air acts will impose significant costs on individuals, although these are likely to be more difficult to quantify than the costs imposed on businesses. Individual smokers who find that the costs of eating out have risen for them, or who find themselves treated like second-class citizens in the workplace, are harmed in a simple and clear-cut manner. The existence of a clean indoor air act brands smokers as social reprobates in the eyes of many who, not having the time or inclination to peruse the technical literature and master its complexities, may trust the assessment of smoking that is rendered by elected officials. This not only will cause smokers undeserved discomfort but will generally tend to reduce the level of civility in society. Such acts add an additional, artificial social conflict between groups of people who would otherwise have no grounds for dispute with one another; that is, they create social conflicts (between smokers and nonsmokers) where otherwise none would exist. By increasing social hostility between smokers and nonsmokers, clean indoor air acts tend to reduce the long-run welfare of both groups. The needless conflict that is created serves no economic purpose and therefore represents pure waste from the standpoint of society as a whole.[6]

The Coase Theorem, Ownership Rights, and Markets

The key idea behind clean indoor air acts is the claim that legally mandated restrictions on the peaceful behavior of individuals acting in markets will increase their welfare. But basic economic theory explains why this common claim is of dubious validity. Where a regime of private property rights prevails, the social costs of ETS are *zero*. Therefore, individuals are *already* maximizing their own welfare (subject to the constraints they face because of the existence of scarcity) without state restrictions on indoor smoking, and the enactment of new restrictions can only make people generally worse off.

Consider the ETS problem in privately owned public places.[7] Bars, restaurants, airlines, and other firms are privately owned entities with residual claimants. In each case, the owner has an economic interest to provide the kind of environment that workers and customers want. For example, firms that hire employees in a competitive labor market will provide certain workplace environments as part of the optimizing compensation package. This may involve smoker–nonsmoker segregation on the job, investment in smoke-removal devices, paying smokers or nonsmokers a wage premium to work in a given environment, and so on. The point is that the owner will internalize the cost of smoking in the workplace.

Suppose that all of a firm's workers prefer to smoke on the job, but the owner of the firm objects strongly to tobacco smoke in the workplace. Clearly, the owner must bear the costs of indulging his preferences. If he requires that his employees not smoke on the job and offers only the going market wage, no one will be willing to work for him. To induce his employees not to smoke, the owner must pay a premium—over and above the competitive wage—that is sufficient to make employment in his firm as attractive as alternative jobs where there are no restrictions on smoking. Alternatively, the owner can offer the market wage, allow smoking on the job, and invest in smoke-removal devices that bring the air quality to his liking. In either case, the costs of imposing a smoking policy are internal to the owner of the firm.

Now, suppose that the owner is indifferent about smoke-filled and smoke-free environments, but some of the workers wish to smoke on the job and others prefer no tobacco smoke in the workplace. How does the owner reconcile these conflicting preferences? There are several alternatives. As before, the owner can ban smoking and pay a wage premium to smokers. Similarly, he can allow smoking on the job and compensate nonsmokers. Other options would be to segregate smoking and nonsmoking employees or to install smoke-removal equipment. Which of these options is chosen will depend on such factors as the mix of smokers and nonsmokers in the firm's workforce, the cost and effectiveness of air cleaners, and the nature of the firm's production process. This last consideration involves the extent to which co-workers can be separated without adverse effects on overall productivity. Market forces will lead the owner to select the smoking policy that achieves the desired result at minimum cost. In a competitive market, we would therefore expect to observe a variety of smoking policies adopted across firms, each of which is optimal for the given circumstances.

Exactly the same argument applies to the owner of a restaurant, bar, or any other private firm that serves a public composed of smokers and nonsmokers. The market for dining out, for example, will discipline firms in the restaurant industry to provide preferred eating and drinking environments. This involves the mechanisms mentioned previously: smoker–non-smoker segregation, smoke-removal devices, price–environment trade-offs, and so on. If the owner bans smoking, smokers will patronize the establishment only if the price–quality combination offered is as attractive as that in alternative eating places where smoking *is* allowed.[8] The opposite applies for nonsmokers if smoking is permitted. And the owner can indulge his own preferences at a cost. Thus, a variety of smoking policies will arise in the marketplace; in the process, the social costs of smoking in restaurants and bars will be minimized.

In other words, with private property and residual claimants in place, the social costs of public smoking are approximately zero. In the case of publicly owned facilities—managed not by residual claimants but by government bureaucrats with little motive to

provide workers or consumers a smoking–nonsmoking environment consistent with their preferences—the situation is admittedly
not subject to the same salutary incentive effects. But even in
publicly owned buildings, market forces can be expected to operate
in a manner that minimizes the social costs of ETS. Government
agencies must compete for workers with private firms, which, as we
have seen, have strong incentives to provide employees with a work
environment consistent with their smoking preferences. Therefore,
those agencies either must provide similar accommodations to *their*
employees, compensating them with a wage premium identical to
what they could receive in the private sector, or they will be unable
to attract suitable workers.[9]

Consumers who need to visit the facilities of a monopoly government bureau (for example, the registry of motor vehicles) may
superficially seem less fortunate, given that such a nonprofit public
monopoly will have little or no incentive to provide a preferred
environment to its "customers." But in the case of ETS exposure, this
is fortunately a trivial problem. Even the most ardent critics of ETS
admit that brief, occasional exposure has not been shown to affect the
health of nonsmokers. Although it may annoy nonsmokers to be
forced to wait in a smoke-filled registry of motor vehicles, no one
argues that it has any proven effect on their health.[10]

Thus, even if we assume that ETS exposure can affect the health
of nonsmokers adversely, rational adults operating in competitive
markets will prevent uncompensated harm from occurring to
anyone. Of course, some nonsmokers may be less risk-averse (and
hence more tolerant of those around them who smoke cigarettes)
than some opponents of tobacco consumption may consider wise.
But one important feature of a free society is that it affords
individuals protection from busybodies who feel themselves quali-
fied to enforce their own personal preferences on others.[11]

The Coase Theorem and Parental Responsibility

As we have seen, the Coase theorem implies that net externalities
associated with ETS are zero. Individual nonsmokers take the
expected cost of exposure to ETS into account when deciding how
to allocate their time and other resources. Continuing exposure to

ETS reflects a decision on the part of the nonsmoker that the marginal benefit he derives from continuing to associate with smokers at least equals the marginal cost. In other words, nonsmokers voluntarily expose themselves to ETS because they judge themselves better off by doing so than they would otherwise be if they avoided smokers. Consequently, all relevant costs to the health of the nonsmoker are fully internalized.

The situation becomes more complex when children are involved. Adults are rational and self-responsible and are fully capable of making their own voluntary decisions and contracting (both formally and informally) with others. But children are, by definition, dependent on adults and cannot be held responsible for their own actions. This is particularly true for very young children, who are totally dependent on their parents in virtually all respects. It would clearly be meaningless to claim that the exposure of children to ETS reflects their rational assessment of the relative costs and benefits of so doing, and that therefore such exposure is a voluntary act on their part. The relevant decision maker in such instances would be not the child but the responsible adult with custody of that child.

This is admittedly a difficult problem, and it deserves to be carefully considered.[12] However, much broader questions are involved. The exposure of children to ETS presents thorny problems, but it is only one member of the large genus of similar problems involving relationships between parents and children. If ETS exposure increases the risks to a child's health, so do other events and activities that commonly occur; for instance, every time a child accompanies his mother to the grocery store, the risk of "automobile accident exposure" dramatically increases. In fact, it is probably true that most activities parents cause their children to engage in increase, to some extent, the risks to the child's health. Exposure to ETS may be more or less risky than some other activities to the health of affected children, but it is not a unique source of risk.

The most crucial consideration seems to be, if children cannot be considered self-responsible, who is responsible for them? The obvious answer is their parents. Parents voluntarily decide what level of ETS exposure is appropriate for their offspring, whether it is generated by themselves or by others. There is naturally a tension between the individual liberty of the parents and the individual liberty of their children. When does the protection of the child interfere with the rights of its parents? At what point does the freedom of a parent to raise his children as he sees fit verge on child abuse? There is no simple answer to these questions. What should be emphasized is the similarity between the exposure to ETS of children by parents and the routine exposure of children by parents to many other risks (some of which are both real and severe)—risks that few would suggest involve violations of the children's individual rights. The problem of the exposure of children to ETS needs to be put into proper perspective.

From an economic perspective, the cost of childrens' exposure to ETS is fully internalized *by their parents*. Parents will decide what level of ETS exposure is appropriate for their children by determining the point at which marginal benefit equals marginal cost. Stated more simply, parents will decide what level of exposure is best for their own children, assuming that there are benefits to be derived from taking part in activities that include smokers. This calculation is no different from that which takes place when parents decide what level of participation in *any* kind of activity is best for their children. In other words, exposure to ETS of a child necessarily involves the voluntary choice of that child's parents.

Finally, let us assume that at some future time it is proved that significant adverse health effects to children came from their exposure to ETS. The appropriate remedy would not then lie in the direction of clean indoor air acts or other measures directed against smokers per se; it would involve sanctioning *parents* for voluntarily exposing their children to ETS. If ETS exposure is regarded as a form of child abuse, it is the parents who expose their children to smoke, not other adult smokers, who ought to be punished.

Tobacco and "Public Health"

In the public debate about environmental tobacco smoke, advocates of legal barriers to smoking continually imply that exposure to smoke is something smokers "do to" nonsmokers. This implication is revealed in language that speaks of nonsmokers "being exposed to" ETS, in contrast to language that speaks of nonsmokers as "exposing themselves to" ETS. This difference in language is important. The former use implies the absence of choice, with exposure to ETS being involuntary. The latter use implies the presence of choice, with exposure to ETS being the result of choice. In the days of the military draft, it might have been accurate to speak of nonsmoking draftees "being exposed to" ETS. But as a general rule in a free society, people "expose themselves to" ETS. To the extent that nonsmokers associate with smokers (and encounter tobacco smoke as a result), this reflects their judgment that the benefits of that association at least equal the costs. All exposure to ETS—most obviously in the case of exposure over a prolonged period, which is when any possible negative health effects might arise—reflects the voluntary choice of the person exposed. In a market economy, individuals will frequently find it to their advantage to have dealings with those whose personal characteristics— whether they involve table manners, personal appearance, bathing habits, or smoking habits—are not entirely pleasing to them. If individuals continue to interact with others who have disagreeable personal characteristics, it must be true that they perceive themselves better off by doing so.

This leads us to the basic problem with "public health" arguments as applied to questions involving smoking in public places. The standard public health paradigm is an external disease that everyone would like to avoid but that is transmitted by invisible organisms and might be spread to innocent victims by means of only a brief exposure to carriers, who may be almost impossible to identify as such (and who may not even know *themselves* that they are infected). In economic terms, the information and the transactions costs associated with identifying and avoiding the disease carriers is sufficiently high to prevent the emergence of efficient market mechanisms that allow the non-infected to protect themselves. For this reason, in some cases it is reasonable to require by law that certain measures be taken (for example, a mandatory quarantine) to prevent the spread of the disease.

But it makes no sense to apply the public health paradigm to the case of ETS. Even if we assume that ETS exposure has been shown, unambiguously, to lead to adverse health consequences for non-smokers, ETS cannot be compared to a disease-carrying organism. Tobacco smoke is clearly visible and gives off a noticeable odor, and lit cigarettes are obvious. Furthermore, unlike exposure to a disease-carrying organism, there are claims in the scientific literature that only a *prolonged* exposure to ETS could possibly harm *anyone*. People may become exposed to smallpox or polio involuntarily and without their knowledge, but prolonged exposure to ETS cannot be anything but the result of *voluntary choice*.

It is an abuse of language to describe ETS exposure—or the consumption of tobacco more generally—as a "disease." The application of grossly inappropriate public health models to questions of smoking regulation represents a substitution of ideology for science. The increasing tendency for disputes between those with different tastes to be transformed into "public health" issues of dubious empirical merit—and the controversy over ETS and the enactment of clean indoor air acts is an excellent example—should be of great concern to those who support institutions consistent with human liberty. The description of activities or behavior by others that some dislike as a "disease" or a "public health menace," on the basis of the limited and contradictory evidence, is an expression of the increasing politicization of society, whereby private disputes (which could be settled spontaneously and amicably by the relevant parties) become objects of unrestrained political conflict. Disputes formerly resolved efficiently through the efforts of profit-seeking entrepreneurs in private markets have increasingly become battlefields across which rent-seeking interest groups struggle for political favoritism. The appeal to the "public's health" is essentially just political rhetoric designed to camouflage naked force. That appeal is not based on science; rather it represents *scientism*—the articulation of scientific-sounding rationalizations to support the use of coercion.[13] The transition of the ETS question from a minor dispute settled peacefully and civilly by market forces to a violent conflict (which is both unnecessary and wasteful) oriented toward using the mechanism of political force is a sorry example of the politicization of modern society at its most grotesque.

Notes

1. For instance, in an effort to portray to smokers the benefits they could derive from quitting, Oster, Colditz, and Kelly (1984) attempted to develop individual-level calculations of the various costs smokers impose upon themselves.
2. See the National Research Council (1986) study, which found no consistent evidence of any linkage between heart disease (p. 265) or cancers other than lung cancers (p. 255) and ETS exposure, some limited evidence of a link between lung cancer and long-term exposure to ETS (based on statistical studies of married couples in which only one spouse smoked) (pp. 245–46), and data suggestive of increased lung and respiratory infections in children whose parents are smokers (pp. 216–17). The report placed great confidence in data pointing to a link between repeated ETS exposure over long periods of time for nonsmoking pregnant women and low-birthweight infants (p. 273).
3. See Coase (1960). Briefly, the Coase theorem suggests that interactions will have efficient outcomes so long as people are free to enter into voluntary contractual agreement.
4. Proposition P in San Francisco was the first clean indoor air act that neither was limited in the range of places covered nor simply required the separation of smokers from nonsmokers (as opposed to prohibition of smoking).
5. Other potential costs arise from the same causes mentioned here. Obviously, as restaurants lose business, they will be forced to lay off workers, and unemployment will increase. Also, tax revenue will be reduced as a function of the reduction in restaurant revenues.
6. For a more detailed discussion of the waste resulting from such artificially created conflict, see Den Uyl (1986).
7. Much of the following argument is drawn from Shughart and Tollison (1986). Describing a privately owned business as a "public place" is very apt, despite the fact that it is in a sense misleading. Obviously, it is really the *owner's* place. Customers and/or employees enter the premises only at their own request and of their own free will. This would be true even if the private business in question had significant monopoly power—for example, if it was the only restaurant in town. But the overwhelming majority of industries that serve the public—and in particular the restaurant industry—are actually *intensely* competitive; owners have no hope of extracting monopoly rents from their customers either by charging excessive prices or by not providing smoking/nonsmoking accommodations in accord with the preferences of the public. Not only is there likely to be another restaurant across the street that is eager to take the customer away by charging a lower price and/or offering better service, but in many cases there will be *dozens* of equally eager restaurants within a few blocks. In a competitive market, a privately owned business is literally a "public place" in the sense that the owner has no discretion in his decision making; if he fails to provide the quality of service consumers demand at a competitive price, he faces bankruptcy. For exactly this reason, the vision of restaurant owners intentionally

snubbing customers by refusing to provide optimal smoking/nonsmoking arrangements is ludicrous.

8. In other words, smokers will consider the marginal benefits and costs of different restaurants in making their choice of which establishment to visit, and they will take into account all factors relevant to them—the decor, the cuisine, the prices of meals, the provisions for smoking, and many others.

9. Admittedly, government managers are not residual claimants in the same sense that private entrepreneurs are; therefore, they will have less incentive to search for and retain competent workers than private firms have. However, although this will tend to reduce the efficiency of public as compared to private enterprises in the delivery of similar services, even public bureaucratic managers are likely to lose their jobs if they fail to maintain a workforce of adequate size and with the minimum skills required to perform their assigned tasks. Therefore, even government enterprises are forced to provide working conditions and salaries that are competitive with those offered by private firms.

10. In the case of government monopolies, the absence of smoking–nonsmoking arrangements that are optimal from the perspective of consumers is only one kind of inefficiency likely to be generated. Government monopolies tend to be grossly inefficient providers of goods and services to consumers, and their managers tend to have no effective incentive to satisfy consumer demand. The solution to the ETS problem in government offices—to the extent that there is one—is not enacting a clean indoor air act but eliminating the inefficient government monopoly and allowing competitive markets to provide goods and services wherever possible. Unlike a clean indoor air act, this solution treats the cause, not just a symptom, and it would also tend to reduce many other serious inefficiencies that plague consumers.

11. Buchanan (1986) has observed that in the end, busybodies may be their own worst enemies by promoting institutional arrangements that may come back to haunt them. Let those who would use the political process to impose their preferences on the behavior of others be wary of the threat to their own liberties, considering the components of their own behavior that might also be subjected to control and regulation. The apparent costlessness of restricting the liberties of others through politics is deceptive. The liberties of some cannot readily be restricted without limiting the liberties of all.

12. Obviously, to the extent that perceived health risks associated with exposure to ETS influence individuals' calculations of the costs and benefits of certain forms of behavior, the economic problem and the medical problem interact. Individuals will make economic decisions on the basis of perceived costs, which include estimated scientific risks.

13. See Buchanan (1986), pp. 340–41.

6
Tobacco Taxation and Regulation in a Public Choice Perspective

W e concluded chapter 4 by observing that the various proposals to earmark tobacco tax revenues for the support of Medicare are better understood by political considerations than by any principles of equity or efficiency. More generally in this vein, we have suggested several times that political processes follow a economic logic and therefore that the outcomes of political processes often conform quite poorly to the values and norms that are commonly presumed to inform policy discourse. In this chapter and the next, we explore more fully this cleavage that often separates normative or value statements about public policy from the empirical consequences of the policy measures that are actually enacted.

Tobacco Taxation and Social Cost: The Case of an Analytical Unicorn

The use of taxation as a tool for social control leads us back to the problem of social cost. Virtually all rationalizations for the taxation of specific goods and services are based on a presumption that voluntary exchange can impose damages on third parties. In light of this presumption, the proper role of government is to force private decision makers, through "corrective" taxation and regulation, to bear the full cost of their activities. As we saw in chapter 5, however, the language of social cost often serves more as an instrument of political advocacy than as a meaningful category of economic analysis. Such costs do not have prices associated with them and hence are not measurable. Because they are not measurable, social costs can easily become analytical "unicorns"—interesting hypothetical situations of little relevance to the real world. Furthermore, even if it were somehow established that an activity generates a cost of $X to some third party, this does not imply that eliminating that cost would be economically efficient, because the effort to do so might cost more than it gains. To the extent that alleged external costs continue to exist over time, it becomes increasingly likely that it would cost the parties involved more to alter the situation than they would gain by doing so. In short, people who support increased taxation of tobacco products should look elsewhere to rationalize their policy preferences, because claims of social cost are too deeply steeped in mythology to withstand critical scrutiny.

Even if the weaknesses of arguments grounded on the concept of social cost are set aside, the case for discriminatory taxation of tobacco products is weak. The costs of smoking are private costs borne by smokers. The alleged social costs generated by smokers evaporate upon careful scrutiny. As we saw in chapter 5, this is so even if it is accepted that there are adverse health consequences for nonsmokers as a result of working or otherwise associating with smokers. In a free society, people choose those with whom they associate. The persons with whom an individual spends time are those whose association produces marginal utility at least equal to marginal cost. The marginal cost of associating with others includes such factors as bad body odor, stupid jokes, poor taste in clothes, and innumerable other personal characteristics that we may not find to our liking. An additional factor that is relevant to some people is whether the other person is a smoker. If a person continues to associate voluntarily with a smoker, either in the workplace or elsewhere, the benefits that person derives from that association must be assumed to exceed its costs. Smoking is no different from a number of other forms of personal behavior in this sense. The same calculus applies—Is this association worth the costs to me?— in cases involving the dressing, drinking, driving, and cursing behavior of others, as well as all other facets of personal behavior that some may find objectionable.

The usual rationalizations for selective taxation as a tool for increasing economic efficiency (by forcing individuals to bear the social costs of their activities) and as a means for paternalistic protection of the "unwashed" from their "vices" are not only weak in and of themselves but are also inconsistent with the liberal values on which a free society is based. Americans in particular have traditionally been extremely skeptical of government as a Big Nanny, and in this context, the usual arguments justifying selective taxes on goods such as cigarettes represent a weak basis for such taxes. This leads to the inevitable conclusion that the rationalizing rhetoric of selective taxation covers up more plausible motivations for such taxes.

What, then, can we infer about the use of such taxes? Are selective excise taxes, which are rationalized by fallacious arguments about social correction, simply the result of mistaken reasoning? To some extent, simple intellectual confusion may contribute to the support for such discriminatory levies, but unless we are willing to abandon the assumption that individuals are rational maximizers—that is, that people in general are not systematically stupid—confusion alone is not plausible as a complete explanation. As economists, we need to ask who gains from discriminatory excise taxes and who loses?

The answer is fairly clear and can be summarized by paraphrasing the Golden Rule: He who has the gold makes the rules. Smoking is more customary among the working class and the poor; lawyers, college professors, and legislators are not usually smokers. Smoking is like bowling—it tends to be a lower-class leisure time activity. But unlike bowling, which nonbowlers largely ignore (perhaps because it is practiced only in bowling alleys), smoking is often conducted in public places and hence offends the sensibilities of many upper-income people. It is irrelevant *why* their sensibilities are offended. They may believe that their own health is harmed by the smoking of others, or that smokers need to be protected from themselves, or simply that smoking is gauche, aesthetically unappealing, and unfashionable. Rules prohibiting smoking in public places are an effective means of discrimination without violating antidiscrimination laws; discriminatory excise taxes on cigarettes help to ensure that "those" people behave "properly." A specific excise tax on polyester clothing would serve the same function, protecting the fashionable from the "bad taste" of the poor.

Unfortunately for them, smokers are a relatively easy target for excise taxation. They face high organization costs with relatively meager resources as a group to fight taxation. Perhaps more important, they have been so thoroughly educated about the supposed social irresponsibility of smoking that guilt prevents them from mounting a determined resistance to tax discrimination. This politically immobilizing guilt, carefully cultivated by the opponents of smoking, helps to explain why poll data indicate that, at any given time, large numbers of current smokers claim to be trying to quit. It is only natural to prefer to be viewed as a victim of a bad habit than as an intentional social reprobate.

This relative vulnerability is exploited by politicians, whose aim is always to increase tax revenues because revenue is the primary raw material for the wealth transfers that have become government's principal activity. In contrast to smokers, other potentially taxable groups of citizens who have higher incomes and are better organized politically can impose higher costs on politicians who seek to tax them. Truck drivers, waitresses, carpenters, and welfare recipients who smoke have little clout. The exploitation of relatively vulnerable groups such as smokers with discriminatory taxation increases political revenue at the margin over what it would be in the absence of such discriminatory exploitation.

Thus, discriminatory excise taxes on tobacco products accomplish two distinct but consistent ends. One is that such duties help keep people with offensive tastes in line, reducing their tendency to engage in distasteful and unfashionable activities that offend the same people who regard bowling alleys as museums of primitive culture. The other is that the revenue from such taxes can be extracted at relatively low political cost by legislators who have insatiable demands to fund transfers to special-interest groups. The fashion-mongering snobs and the rent-seeking politicos form an unholy alliance, the outcome of which is the imposition of a highly regressive tax on those with lower incomes, for the different but compatible purposes of social control and revenue maximization.

An Economic Approach to Legislation and Regulation

Legislation as an Economic Process

For almost two hundred years, it was common for most economists to assume that the realm of economics was the wide world outside the hall of the legislature and the other offices of government. Private interest ruled the economic world, but the decision making of government was guided by the public interest, which was calculated by selfless public servants who constantly strove to improve the welfare of society. The revolution in economics known as *public choice* changed all this. The decision making of government was now admitted to be part of the economic universe. Government officials were recognized as being neither better nor worse than ordinary private citizens and as being motivated by neither more nor less noble goals.

One of the most important developments to arise from the public choice revolution has been the extension of economic analysis to the process by which legislation is actually produced in legislatures. A growing literature has shown that the process of legislating by a legislature can be effectively modeled as the output of a kind of market, with unusual characteristics to be sure, but nevertheless conforming to the same economic principles as production in more ordinary kinds of markets.[1]

For better or for worse, legislatures are a kind of marketplace. Legislators supply output in the form of legislation to demanders who bid against one another for bills in a kind of auction. These demanders are various interest groups that may represent huge industries, or major labor unions, or individual companies, or even individuals seeking a tax break. The legislation supplied—that is, the bills actually passed—is thus not the result of some Olympian deliberation by white-robed, selfless legislators, but the result of vigorous competitive bargaining and haggling in which interest groups bid against one another for legislative favor. The actual process of legislating bears little resemblance to the accounts presented in high school civics classes; but the more accurate view, based on economic analysis, is not cynical, just more realistic.

Most would agree that many laws passed as the result of this competitive bidding process among interest groups are effective and serve important purposes that enhance the welfare of society. Unhappily for the welfare of society, other bills pass the legislature as well—bills that simply transfer wealth from taxpayers to favored interest groups in one way or another and, in the process, reduce economic efficiency and therefore harm social welfare. These are the bills that undertake to do such things as establish mandatory licensing for barbers, which serves not to protect the public but only to protect present barbershop owners from future competition. Real-world legislatures pass numerous laws that erect entry barriers, establish legal monopolies, subsidize certain activities at taxpayer expense, and in other ways generate financial gain for favored interest groups while harming the interests of society at large. By enacting measures of this kind, legislatures produce wealth transfers at the expense of wealth creation and lower the efficiency of the overall economy.[2]

Wealth Transfers versus Wealth Creation

There are two major categories of economic activity. The one that has traditionally interested economists involves the creation of wealth through the pursuit of gains from trade. This form of economic activity represents a gain in welfare for all participants. In a free market context, all economic activity increases the perceived wealth of the voluntary participants; otherwise, they would not engage in the activity. Some wealth will take a physical and tangible form (for example, iron ore mined from the ground), while other wealth will take forms that are less tangible and much harder to measure, such as increases in the satisfaction of consumers (for example, the increased well-being supplied to parents as the result of baby-sitting services) or improvements in organization that permit the more efficient use of scarce resources. Legislative activity that improves the security of contracts, makes the enforcement and adjudication of the law more efficient, or otherwise helps to make market exchange less costly also represents wealth creation.

The other form of economic activity, wealth transfer, does not represent mutual gain; rather, it represents one person gaining at someone else's expense. Rather than becoming wealthier through providing a service of value to someone else, wealth is acquired by taking *someone else's* wealth. The paradigm of wealth transfer activity is pocket picking. Anyone who has read Dickens is aware of the investment in specialized training, the rational weighing of risks versus benefits, and the general businesslike attitude of the successful pickpocket. Picking pockets for profit is just as much a rational, deliberate economic activity as running a steel mill or selling greeting cards. But unlike those involved in these other activities, the pickpocket does not increase the net wealth of society; he just transfers the wealth created by someone else to himself. Also, to make matters worse, pocket picking causes the net wealth of society to *decrease* by the amount of the pickpocket's investment of time and resources in his profession as well as the investment by potential victims to protect their wallets, both of which are pure waste from the standpoint of society.

We do not deny that morality may play an important role in curbing outright thievery; those who refrain from theft do so as the result of their moral training and belief that stealing is wrong. Nonetheless, an individual's decision to engage in wealth transfer instead of wealth creation (or vice versa) is economically understandable without making moral assumptions. People specialize in different activities because they have different talents, interests, and abilities; and those things that allow the individual to earn the highest return will be different for different individuals. Economists refer to this phenomenon as the law of comparative advantage. Some people will earn the highest return they can as plumbers, others as architects. Some will earn the most as doctors, others as pickpockets. And of direct relevance to our concerns here, some will have a comparative advantage in actively competing for profit in the marketplace, while others will have a comparative advantage in lobbying for transfers in the legislature.

Democratic Politics and Tax Policy

The economic theory of legislation provides a basis for understanding both the process by which tax policy is enacted in a democracy and the outcomes of that process. The legislature is viewed not as a selfless and dedicated servant of something called "public interest" but rather as a set of ordinary people pursuing activities that offer the highest rewards. The realities of tax policy formation as one subset of legislative outcomes contrast sharply with the various normative theories of taxation that are often touted by those who feel that taxes should be employed by government as tools for social engineering. Progressive tax rate structures have often been defended on the basis that the capitalist free market system, when left alone, will generate an inequitable distribution of income; government ought to step in and restore fairness by taxing the rich at higher rates and redistributing the revenue to the poor, thereby making the income distribution more equal.[3] Another, related view holds that government should tax the rich at higher rates because the marginal utility of money diminishes as wealth increases; one more dollar may be of inconsequential importance to a millionaire but may make the difference between making the rent or getting tossed out on the street to a poor person (an intuitively plausible view that most economists reject as being based on invalid intuition).[4]

When these claims concerning the nature of a just tax system are compared with reality, an obvious chasm appears. Virtually all loopholes in the form of exemptions and deductions benefit middle- and upper-income individuals. At the same time, current tax law places substantial impediments on the efforts of the poor to become self-supporting and self-sufficient. Of course, it is meaningless to look only at the net tax burden without taking into account the *consumption* of tax revenues. If a particular group pays $X in annual taxes but the government spends $X + N on that group subsequently, the group is net tax *consumer* in the amount $N.

The current tax system not only directly increases the poverty problem but also increases the difficulties the poor face in attempting to pull themselves out of poverty. Blank and Blinder (1986) reported that according to census calculations in 1982, the combined effects of federal, state, and local taxes pushed the income of 3.2 million taxpayers below the federal poverty threshold. According to Pechman (1985), the average rate of tax by states and localities on families in the lowest 10 percent of the income distribution actually rose from 1966 to 1985 (due mostly to increases in the level of excise taxes). Danziger and Gottschalk (1985) found that the effective federal tax rate facing the poor (defined as total federal tax as a percentage of family income) increased from only 1.3 percent in 1975 to 10.1 percent in 1984. The combined effects of federal, state, and local taxation reduce the effective earnings of the working poor and reduce their incentives to leave welfare programs by moving up the economic ladder.

Rent Seeking, Tax Resistance, and Social Waste

Review of the Excess Burden Literature

When the government collects a dollar in revenue from a tax on tobacco products, the disposable income of consumers is reduced by one dollar. However, the burden the tax imposes on the economy will exceed the amount of tax revenue collected by the government. The additional burden represents a social waste in the sense that it represents value forgone—that is, it does not go to anyone. This waste is usually termed the excess burden, or deadweight cost, due to the tax.

As outlined in chapter 2, this deadweight cost results from the differential between the price per pack of cigarettes after the tax and the value to consumers of alternative forms of output relative to an additional pack of cigarettes. If the cost of an additional pack of cigarettes with the tax is $1.20 and the cost in terms of alternative output forgone to produce that pack is 80 cents (which in a free market will tend to be equal to the pretax price), consumers are made worse off *beyond* the 40 cent tax ($1.20 − $0.80 = $0.40) by the extent to which the value they place on additional cigarettes exceeds the cost of producing those additional cigarettes. This is the excess burden; it is the lost utility consumers *would* have received if they had been permitted to purchase a quantity of cigarettes up to the point at which the value of the last cigarette to them equaled its cost of production.

An important corollary to the theory of excess burden is commonly cited in the case of tobacco taxation: The magnitude of the excess burden associated with a tax on a specific commodity will tend to be inversely related to the elasticity of demand for that commodity. Hence, the excess burden resulting from a tax on a commodity subject to a very elastic demand (for example, newspapers) will tend to be relatively high, whereas the excess burden resulting from a tax on an inelastically demanded commodity (for example, cigarettes) will be relatively low. This is because the more inelastic the demand for the good, the less likely it is that the tax will have any effect on consumer behavior. A tax on newspapers will cause many consumers to shift to substitutes (they will listen to the radio, watch TV, or buy weekly newsmagazines). The shift to these available substitutes, which provide the consumer with lower satisfaction than newspapers did at the pretax price, will create a significant deadweight cost. In contrast, because few close substitutes are available for cigarette smokers, the tax will have relatively little impact on their consumption choices; consequently, the aggregated deadweight cost of this tax will be relatively low.

This is the conventional account of the social waste resulting from excise taxation. In recent years, however, economists have begun to recognize that the conventional account ignores an important source of additional tax-related social loss and therefore seriously underestimates the true magnitude of the total social waste resulting from excise taxation. This additional source of inefficiency is the rent-seeking loss.

Rent Seeking in General

One of the propositions of economics best understood by the general public is that profits associated with a given business activity will inspire competition by other suppliers that are eager to earn profits for themselves. If Acme Pest Control invests in and markets a better mousetrap and thereby receives large profits, other pest-control firms will strive to market similar (or even superior) products to consumers in order to take away some of Acme's profits for themselves. As a result of this competition, motivated by simple self-interest on the part of competing firms, consumers benefit from better and cheaper mousetraps, to say nothing of the similar benefits from millions of other goods and services. The market economy, with its enormous productivity and inventiveness, is rooted in the profit-seeking endeavors of individuals and firms.

One of the important developments that has arisen out of the public choice revolution during the past twenty-five years has been the extension of the same basic paradigm of economic analysis to the political realm. The political process is not somehow magically insulated from the economic world; it operates according to the same basic principles. The reason for this is that politics is populated by the same self-interested, rational, maximizing individuals who populate the ordinary marketplace. The theory of public choice represents the extension of the profit-seeking paradigm to the political realm, and the theory of rent seeking is an important subset of the theory of public choice, for it is concerned with explaining the wealth-transferring activities of government.

The key relevant proposition here is that all governmental decisions and policies tend to transfer wealth within society. Simply stated, any government action creates winners and losers. This will be true even of policies that are not explicitly designed to redistribute wealth. Rent-seeking analysis emphasizes that economic actors will invest resources in competition for these wealth transfers (or rents) in much the same way that business enterprises compete for consumer dollars.

Rent-seeking activity will have an important consequence in terms of the excess burden associated with a particular tax or regulation. As we noted in chapter 2, according to the conventional analysis, excess burden would be approximately equal to one-half the product of the increase in price and the decrease in output brought about by the tax. But this understates the amount of wasted resources associated with the tax or regulation. All resources invested—by both those in favor and those opposed—in lobbying about the measure in question are also a pure waste from the standpoint of society as a whole. These resources have been devoted not to efforts to increase the stock of wealth but only to efforts to affect the process by which a portion of the existing stock of wealth is reallocated. Thus, these resources have been lost to the productive economy. As we argued earlier, in the end, this rent-seeking investment will be equal to the expected value of the wealth transfer resulting from the tax or regulation. Hence, the potential excess burden from a tax is much higher than conventionally measured, for tax revenues raised by the tax can also be a gauge of the extent of social costs.

Rent Seeking Applied to Tax Resistance

As the preceding discussion suggests, the existence of a transfer rent implies not only that potential recipients will make some level of investment in competing for that rent, but also that the potential victims will make some investment to prevent or at least reduce that transfer. Both the offensive pursuit of rents through legislation and the defensive effort to avoid losing rents through the rent-seeking efforts of others are rational economic activities that stem from the ability of the legislature to transfer wealth through taxation and regulation. It must be recognized that the ability of those adversely affected by government-imposed restrictions to engage in defensive, contra-rent-seeking activity is vital to the protection of their rights and liberties in a free society. Nevertheless, from a strict economic perspective, in the short run, such investment is analytically equivalent to rent seeking.

But when anti-rent-seeking, tax-resistance activity—like rent seeking, a net waste from the standpoint of society—is taken into account, the conventional claim that a tax on the most inelastically demanded goods or services is the least wasteful tax becomes dubious. Consumers will be most likely to organize to fight a tax imposed on the most inelastically demanded goods. A commodity for which the demand is highly elastic is one for which good substitutes are readily available. The imposition of a tax on such a commodity will lead consumers to shift readily to the nontaxed alternative product that is nearly as satisfactory as the taxed product. The availability of such alternative products reduces the potential gain from tax resistance. By contrast, a commodity for which demand is inelastic is one that has no close substitutes. In this case, consumers will have more to gain from resisting the tax through political activity.

At the same time, suppliers of commodities for which demand is highly elastic are unlikely to be earning supranormal profits. Because of the availability of close substitutes for the output they produce, they will be unable to set price above the marginal cost of production. Since they are not earning supranormal profits (rents), they have minimal incentive and resources to organize themselves to oppose the tax. But the suppliers of inelastically demanded goods will probably be able to set price *above* marginal cost, because close substitutes are *not* available. Because they will therefore be earning supranormal profits (rents), they will have an incentive to invest resources to defeat (or reduce) the tax that would reduce the magnitude of this rent flow.

When the demand for a commodity is relatively elastic, neither consumers nor producers are likely to have an incentive to invest significant resources in efforts either to prevent the imposition of a proposed excise tax or to eliminate an existing tax. But when the demand is relatively inelastic, both consumers and producers will have a stronger incentive to invest in opposing the tax or increases in it. When this is taken into account, it becomes problematic whether excise taxes on elastically demanded goods (with low anti-rent-seeking investment but large excess burden) or on inelastically demanded goods (with high anti-rent-seeking investment but low excess burden) will generate greater social waste. In some cases, taxing inelastically demanded commodities (such as tobacco products) will tend to generate the maximum social loss.[5]

The Social Cost of Tobacco Taxation: A Recalculation

The foregoing argumentation suggests that the conventional analysis of the excess burden that results from taxes—in particular, cigarette taxes—grossly understates the true economic cost of the tax. As noted in chapter 2, what is often claimed as the excess burden resulting from the taxation of cigarettes is about 7 percent of the revenue raised by the tax. But the full potential extent of the excess burden also includes the revenue raised by the tax. This is because the entire amount of the transfer of wealth associated with the tax will be up for grabs and rent-seeking interest groups will invest up to this amount in competition for it. Consequently, the total amount of excess burden when rent-seeking costs are included could exceed the amount of revenue the government generates from the tax. In terms of the numerical illustration used in chapter 2, the government's revenue will be limited to $11.2 billion ($0.40 × 28 billion packs sold), but the total excess burden plus rent-seeking loss could be as high as $12 billion ($11.2 billion + $800 million excess burden).

In practice, it is unlikely that the total waste resulting from a tax will reach this magnitude. Efforts to influence legislative outcomes are subject to significant transaction costs as compared with ordinary markets, and the greater uncertainty that thus results will tend to lower the level of rent-seeking investment somewhat. But even if these costs are likely to be somewhat smaller than our simplified example implies, they will nevertheless tend to be large.

Economic Principles and the Anticancer Bureaucracy

Economic Principles of Bureaucratic Conduct

A government bureau may superficially seem to be the opposite of a business firm in a market economy and, hence, necessarily impervious to economic analysis. On the surface, a bureaucracy is a hierarchy ruled from top to bottom, with all decisions being made centrally and with members acting on orders from their superiors, not through voluntary exchange. Even some economists have used the bureaucracy as an example of the antithesis of the marketplace.

In recent years, however, a number of economists have succeeded in extending economic analysis to the decision-making process within bureaucracies. Although such organizations are not markets in the ordinary sense—that is, they are not characterized by competition within the context of explicit prices for goods and services—they do function, nonetheless, according to ordinary economic principles.

A bureau differs from a private firm in one important respect; unlike a firm, a bureau does not have profits that can be directly appropriated by owners. This is a major difference to be sure; nevertheless, there are major similarities between the two types of organization. There are powerful incentives in each for managers to act in ways that increase the relative power of the organization at large. Managers in firms are rewarded with promotions and increased salaries when they increase the firm's profits by expanding sales. Bureaucratic managers are similarly rewarded with promotions and increased salaries when they succeed in expanding the "sales" of their bureau in terms of its political influence and public support. Larger bureaucratic organizations tend to provide higher rates of pay and perquisites to management. Also, the political influence of a bureau— as well as its ability to serve interest groups that can reward management with promises of lucrative future contracts or employment, if not actual bribes—tends to be a function of its size. For these reasons, government bureaus tend to be dominated by the economic interests of their management and to behave in economically predictable—though often inefficient—ways.[6]

The Anticancer Bureaucracy in a Public Choice Perspective

The debate about the regulation and taxation of smoking is intimately related to various claims concerning the alleged adverse health consequences associated with smoking. Essentially, all of the opposition to smoking is ultimately based on various claims regarding these alleged consequences. The most important of these claims involve the alleged relationship between cigarettes and cancer.

All facts (or purported facts) concerning the alleged links between smoking and cancer are produced by the cancer research community, which includes both private and public establishments and which is heavily subsidized by the federal government. Because of the enormous level of federal government involvement in this research, it is useful to describe this research establishment as a single bureaucracy, even though a number of distinct private and public organizations are involved.

Although it may seem obvious that these principles of bureaucratic behavior should apply to units such as the Registry of Motor Vehicles or the Department of Defense, some might balk at the logical extension of them to such other units as the cancer research bureaucracy, by which we refer to government bureaucracies such as the National Institutes of Health as well as private-sector organizations such as the American Cancer Society and various other foundations and research institutes. But the economic principles of bureaucracy are as applicable to these agencies as they are to other agencies more commonly considered "bureaucratic."

As they apply to the anticancer bureaucracy, the economic principles of bureaucracy suggest that, as compared with organization through market competition, the anticancer bureaucracy will face weaker incentives to find and develop effective treatments of and cures for cancer and will face incentives to exaggerate the risks of cancer. The first point is more subtle than merely noting that a cure for cancer would put many cancer bureaucrats out of work, even though a consideration of such perverse incentives has led at least one critic of the medical establishment to suggest that the cancer bureaucracy is the last place to look for a cancer cure.[7] There are, of course, several occupations that depend on a continuation of a state of affairs that its practitioners seek to eliminate but for which universal success would end the occupation. Divorce lawyers and family counselors would go out of business if people were to learn how to get along together. Physicians might advise people how to stay healthy, but healthy people would have little demand for physicians. In these and related cases, what provides the incentive for individual practitioners to promote the interests of their clients— an incentive that clashes somewhat with the interests of the entire group of practitioners—is the competitive organization of service delivery.

There is clearly competition among cancer researchers, but those researchers are in a somewhat different position from ordinary market competitors. Competitors must always seek to please their customers. In ordinary market arrangements, these customers are numerous and decentralized. It would be the same with cancer research if the sponsors of that research were numerous and decentralized, but such sponsorship is centralized and largely monopolized. Although individual researchers have incentives to find cures for cancer, they also have incentives to please their sponsors—and the dominant sponsor is a government bureaucracy, not the numerous and variegated buyers that constitute a competitive market.

The second point is a mere recognition of the application of individual profit incentives in a nonprofit setting. In bureaus, larger budgets are generally preferred to smaller budgets. One means of gaining larger budgets is to "advertise," as it were. With respect to the cancer bureaucracy, one form such advertisement can take is to exaggerate the incidence and risk of cancer. The most successful the bureaucracy is in portraying an image of the ubiquitousness of cancer, the larger the governmental appropriations and charitable donations will be.

The spurious nature of many recent claims about the risks of cancer that have been made even by prominent researchers was the subject of a book by Efron (1984). She found that even the most absurd claims, with the weakest empirical support, tended to be seized by the public and the media as fact, and that standards of scientific rigor were habitually relaxed, virtually to the point of abandonment, by cancer researchers. Virtually every imaginable substance and practice, both man-made and natural, has been claimed by some representative of one of the major cancer research institutes (either the National Cancer Institute, a federal government agency, or some other institution) to be carcinogenic. This list includes virtually all chemicals known to exist,[8] all forms of energy generation (including solar cells and solar heating and cooling systems),[9] most major components of foods (including salt and sugar),[10] and even numerous naturally occurring substances in the air we breathe (including oxygen itself).[11] The overwhelming majority of these claims are based on flimsy evidence or no evidence at all. Scientists (sometimes even those associated with major cancer research foundations) who held reservations about the validity of some of the more extreme claims made by their colleagues concerning cancer risks expressed reluctance about mentioning those reservations in public for fear of being ostracized or branded as tools of industry.

Again, it is not strictly relevant whether the conscious motives of cancer researchers are pristine and sincere or cynically self-interested. The point is that any increased level of perceived cancer risk among the general public is eventually likely to increase their pecuniary incomes. Efron (1984) concluded that "basic" or "pure" science has been partially supplanted by something she termed "regulatory science":

> In principle, basic science is concerned to explain the biological mechanisms of cancer; its goal is understanding. But "regulatory" science is concerned with the legal elimination of carcinogenic substances in the environment whether biological understanding exists or not. . . . The basic scientist, whether he works for the government or at a university, is an intellectual explorer in search of truth, and coercion is no part of his repertoire. The "regulatory" scientist, whether he works for the government or at a university, is an intellectual policeman whose judgments, if accepted by regulators, are backed up by the guns of the state. (p. 232)

If the "regulatory scientist" is actually an intellectual policeman, there is a simple economic explanation for his unscientific behavior. He is protecting his existing rents in the form of his salary and status, which has been artificially increased by his encouragement of cancer fears that have dubious validity, not to mention his protection of possible increases in future rents resulting from the expected expansion of the cancer bureaucracy. When viewed from the perspective of a competitive marketplace or from that of some notion of public interest, this is a questionable way to run a scientific research establishment, and it is clearly inconsistent with the basic integrity of science as a whole. But when viewed from the perspective of the economic theory of bureaucracy it nonetheless represents perfectly rational behavior.

What Does the Surgeon General Optimize?

We ask this question seriously, though in doing so we look upon the Surgeon General as an example of a wider phenomenon. Although he is not the actual administrator of the National Institutes of Health or any of the other major components of the federal research bureaucracy, he is the chief public representative of a bureaucratic empire that will tend to expand in size and scope as its budget increases. It is obvious that the budget will be functionally related to the perceived risk of cancer and other diseases within the Congress and the general public. It takes neither a Machiavellian imagination nor a Ph.D. in economics to conclude that the Surgeon General has a built-in incentive to exaggerate the risk of cancer.

If the research community were largely independent of government funding, notably including funding from the National Institutes of Health, any statements by the Surgeon General, which should have a strong basis in research findings, would be vulnerable to attack by alert and technically competent critics. But this competitive organization of funding is not even remotely the case. In 1984, the federal government spent $4.3 billion for research, most of it on various forms of cancer; the National Cancer Institute spent about $1 billion.[12] In addition, federal tax policy encourages cancer research in a variety of ways. The Surgeon General is not the actual administrator of this vast research bureaucracy, but he is the chief public spokesman for this bureaucracy's interests. We do not expect employees of General Dynamics to be disinterested, reliable witnesses to the probity and honesty of General Dynamics management. Why should we apply different standards to the medical research community?

The Surgeon General could be described as the nation's chief doctor. He is basically a representative of the interests of the medical profession at large. The medical profession, like all professions, may at times face perverse incentives with regard to the services it provides. Auto mechanics may be expected to exaggerate the mechanical defects present in a car they have been assigned to repair. However, they face the constraint of competition. Auto mechanics compete vigorously, have no national organization designed to limit competition, and are not heavily subsidized by the government in such a manner that they are rewarded for finding more "broken" cars—so the perverse incentives they face are kept under tight control. These controls would seem to be much slacker in the case of medical research because of the dominant position of the government as the purchaser of medical research.

Tobacco Taxation and Regulation:
A Realistic Approach

The antismoking lobby portrays itself as engaging in a crusade to save smokers from themselves and, at the same time, seeking to rescue nonsmokers from the "social costs" imposed on them by smokers. We have argued that the "social cost" justifications for the antismoking crusade are pseudoscience masquerading as economic analysis. It seems unlikely that such specious arguments actually inspire the intellectual commitment of large numbers of rational and articulate people, such as many of those who promote restrictions on smoking.

This leaves us with paternalism as a major motivational factor. But this, too, seems unconvincing. Many of the people in the forefront of the antismoking movement are known for their long-time commitments to civil libertarian positions such as freedom of speech, civil rights, and skepticism of governmental intrusion into the personal lives of individuals in general. Rank paternalism has rarely appealed to Americans, and it seems particularly inconsistent among many of those who are prominently identified with the antismoking movement. The rhetoric used by the antismoking movement seems to have little to do with what the movement is actually about.

As we saw in chapter 5, with private property and residual claimants in place, the social costs of smoking in public are proximately zero. Owners of private establishments have an incentive to provide the kind of environment that is most satisfactory to their customers. Therefore, in the absence of government smoking regulations, private rules concerning smoking, segregation of smokers from nonsmokers, and investment in smoke-removal devices will tend to be economically optimal. Some restaurants will cater to smokers, some to nonsmokers; some businesses will establish a smoke-free workplace, some will not; and private property owners in general will provide the degree of smoke-free environment that their customers and employees most prefer, because only by doing so will they maximize their own profits.

But even if the profit-seeking decisions of private entrepreneurs will tend to provide for an efficient mix of rules regarding smoking and no-smoking, nonsmokers may still stand to gain from making no-smoking rules universal and compulsory. We must face the fact that some people simply do not like the fact that other people smoke, for whatever reason. In the absence of wage effects, which we will consider later, nonsmoking workers may prefer that smoking be banned outright if the price to themselves is low enough. If a nonsmoking worker were to bear the full cost of achieving a smoke-free workplace, he might decide that although he would *ideally* prefer that *no one* smoke, he would actually *choose* a situation in which the cost to him of reducing smoking equals the benefits to him of that reduction. This situation, if we make the usual assumptions about rising marginal cost curves, would probably be one in which some smoking is still permitted. In practice, it will be much more expensive for a business to prohibit smoking altogether than to segregate smokers from nonsmokers or to allow smoking only in designated areas. Nonsmokers may not be willing to bear the cost of such measures (that is, they may be unwilling to accept lower wages in return for company enforcement of nonsmoking rules), but they might still favor legislative action to ban smoking if they perceived that it cost them little or nothing.

Antismoking rules may find support among nonsmoking workers for another reason. There are data suggesting that smokers are relatively efficient workers. In some cases, they have lower rates of absenteeism than nonsmokers.[13] Moreover, a recent study indicated that smokers tend to be relatively more productive workers.[14] And other research has reported that smoking may enhance the ability to concentrate on assigned tasks.[15] Thus, the movement to exclude smokers from the workplace may be motivated, in part, by the fact that nonsmokers can expect to gain in wages by excluding higher-productivity smokers from competing with them in the workplace.

To the extent that no-smoking rules make smokers less productive on the job, as well as less likely to be hired in the first place, the wages of nonsmokers will tend to rise relative to that of smokers. Hence, laws restricting or prohibiting smoking have a simple redistribution basis—they transfer wealth from smokers to nonsmokers. Of course, these gains will be only transitory. In the long run, competition among nonsmokers for jobs will drive wages down to the amount just sufficient for them to accept employment in their preferred workplace environment. In the interim, however, nonsmokers earn rents, and these short-run returns provide a sufficient incentive for them to support no-smoking legislation.

So nonsmokers gain in two ways from no-smoking rules. They obtain a working environment they most prefer at a zero (or very low) price, and they receive restriction rents (at least in the short run) that increase their wages. Nonsmoking consumers tend to benefit in similar ways from smoking bans. Legal restrictions on smoking in bars and restaurants tend to shift the supply curve to the right, which, other things being equal, tends to lower the money price of dining out in a no-smoking atmosphere. Under such conditions, nonsmokers who eat out not only obtain a more preferred environment but enjoy a lower price as well. On the other hand, smokers and restaurant owners lose.[16]

Although there are data suggesting that high-skilled male workers (including white-collar and professional workers) who smoke are relatively more productive than their nonsmoking colleagues, smokers are found disproportionately among the ranks of the lower-skilled, the poor, and the young. The incidence of tobacco taxation tends to fall heavily on lower-income groups, and this burden decreases the disposable income available to poor individuals to allocate to human capital development through education and training for themselves and their children. In consequence, the probability is lessened that such individuals and/or their children will acquire the skills necessary to allow them to enter and compete in the skilled labor force, where they face the best chance for improving their long-run income status. Existing skilled laborers— particularly the members of labor unions—stand to receive reduced wages in the long run as a result of competition with new entrants into the skilled labor force from the ranks of the previously poor and unskilled. Discriminatory taxation imposed on the poor, such as tobacco taxation, tends to function as a form of entry barrier that generates monopoly rents for relatively wealthy skilled workers.

Antismoking measures also tend to function as a form of racial discrimination. A disproportionate share of smokers are black and Hispanic. Measures that discriminate against smokers thus effectively act to discriminate against members of these minority groups. In modern America, overt racial discrimination is prevented by law;

Jim Crow was killed by the civil rights revolution of the 1960s. But antismoking rules allow a form of discrimination against members of minority groups that evades federal and state laws designed to eliminate discrimination along racial lines. A business may not be able to refuse to hire blacks because of their race, but it can legally refuse to hire a black smoker who refuses to quit if the firm has a "no smoking" policy or if the local law requires a "smoke-free" workplace.

Notes

1. See McCormick and Tollison (1981) and Peltzman (1984) for reviews of the literature.
2. For a recent treatise examining how government has become an instrument for acquiring wealth through taking instead of through production, see Epstein (1985).
3. See chapter 12 of Boadway (1979) for a technical summary of these arguments.
4. Although the law of diminishing marginal utility applies to specific goods (a given unit purchased provides less utility to the consumer than the unit purchased before it), it does not apply to goods in general. Money represents command over goods in general. Although, in some individual cases, each additional dollar may generate less utility than the one before it (for example, in the case of a monk), it is possible that in other cases, the utility associated with each additional dollar actually *increases*. Therefore, even if we could measure and compare utility across persons—which is impossible—it is possible that we would find that the additional dollar generated more utility for the millionaire than it did for the chimney sweep. The point is simply that one cannot generalize across people about the value of additional income or command over goods and services.
5. For a more detailed argument, see Lee and Tollison (1985).
6. See Tullock (1965) and Niskanen (1971) for a more detailed analysis.
7. Szasz (1978) has made this observation on numerous occasions.
8. Joseph Califano, then HEW Secretary, put the number at 7 million in 1978. See Efron (1984), p. 97.
9. Ibid., p. 102.
10. Ibid., p. 160.
11. Ibid., p. 166.
12. See Office of Management and Budget (1985), p. I-K4. The total spent by the federal government on all forms of cancer research in 1984 was probably between $2 billion and $3 billion.

13. Solmon (1983) found that, according to the 1976 National Health Survey, smokers of fewer than fifteen cigarettes per day had an absenteeism rate of 2.6 days, compared with 4.3 days for nonsmokers. He also noted that the 1979 Surgeon General's Report showed that male smokers of fewer than eleven cigarettes per day were absent less than nonsmokers and that women aged seventeen and older who were presently smokers had less bed disability than nonsmokers.

14. Dahl, Gunderson, and Kuehnast (1984) studied a group of fifty-five financial managers at Minnesota's Farm Credit Services and found that smokers were significantly more productive than nonsmokers; smokers were found to be 2.5 percent more efficient in allocating their time to assigned tasks.

15. Spielberger (1986) reported the results of a survey given to 425 college students who were current smokers. Respondents' reasons for continuing to smoke included perceived relaxation, stimulation, and the facilitation of thinking aided by smoking.

16. As Shughart and Tollison (1986) concluded:

The interest-group explanation . . . suggests that firms and smokers will generally oppose laws restricting smoking behavior, while nonsmokers advocate them. In particular instances one group wins over the other, depending on such factors as the costs of organizing the respective coalitions and of influencing the political process. In any event, it would appear to be interest groups and wealth transfers and not concern over an externality that drives public policy in this area. (p. 223)

7
Tobacco and Public Policy: A Constitutionalist Perspective

In the traditional, pre–public-choice approach to public policy, the creation of public policy was seen as exogenous to the economic process. Within this exogenous perspective, there was no scope for a theory of economic policy or political choice as such. The analytical task was not to explain the central characteristics of the policy choices that emerge from a political process, but rather to advise the policymaker on the characteristics of desirable policy measures. To this day, the central core of what is called welfare economics has consisted of specifying the characteristics of "good" policy measures. Whoever is the creator of public policy stands outside the economic process, and the task for the economic analyst is to suggest ways for the policymaker to improve the operation of the economic process. Presumably, the more benevolent or public-spirited the policymaker, the more fully the policy measures actually enacted will advance the economic welfare of the nation.

But once the production of public policy is itself treated as an ordinary economic activity, as the public choice approach treats it and as the Founding Fathers did, public policy becomes endogeneous to the economic process, and the characteristics of public policy measures become objects of explanation. In this case, what primarily governs those characteristics are the incentives that politicians face. For a given set of incentives, there will tend to be a particular set of policy measures that will represent a political equilibrium. This statement is equivalent to the proposition that for a given set of preferences, resource availabilities, technologies, and property rights, there will exist an economic equilibrium. In the familiar economic case, we say that for changes in the structure of production to take place, there must be preceding changes in such things as preferences, resource availabilities, technologies, and property rights. But in similar fashion, we can say that changes in the characteristic outcomes of the political process require changes in the same things, but in this case, "property rights" refer to the whole set of institutional rules constraining the operation of political processes.

A constitution, then, is a set of social institutions or rules within which individuals operate and interact with one another. All societies must have some sort of constitution under which social interaction is regulated and disputes between individuals with competing ends are resolved. A society without a constitution is not really a society at all; it is a jumble of individuals at best and a mob at worst. The social constitution is analogous to the rules of the game in sports. Brennan and Buchanan (1980) developed this analogy:

> A game is described by its rules—its constitution. These rules establish the framework within which the playing of the game proceeds; they set boundaries on what activities are legitimate, as well as describing the objects of the game and how to determine who wins. It is clear intuitively that the choice among alternative strategies that a player might make in the course of a game is categorically quite distinct from his prior choice among alternative sets of rules. A tennis player after hitting a particular shot may reasonably wish that the net was lower, yet prior to the game he may have agreed to a set of rules in which the height of the net was specified. (p. 3)

It is important to emphasize that *all* social orders are ultimately based on some sort of constitution. Hence, the social constitution is not necessarily related to the document by that name that often serves as the legal basis for government; the constitution of society in America may be thought to include, but is not the same as, the U.S. Constitution. The social constitution refers to all of the "rules of the game" that affect social interaction and regulate disputes among individuals—not just laws, but also all other relevant social conventions that constrain individual behavior.

A constitutionalist perspective implies that since the production of public policy conforms to an economic logic, "improvement" in the type of policy measures produced is much more a matter of changing the incentives constraining political processes than it is a matter of giving policymakers better advice. For this reason, a constitutionalist perspective focuses on an analysis of social inter-action that explicitly takes into account the constitutional con-straints affecting social behavior and pays particular attention to the effects resulting from changes in these constraints over time. Constitutions are not the result of divine intervention, nor are they laid upon us by exogenous but benevolent despots. Rather, they arise from interactions among utility-maximizing individuals pur-suing their self-interest, each of whom must accommodate to the fact of others' similar actions. Constitutions arise from the pur-posive action of rational, self-interested individuals, not from selfless lawgivers. For this reason, constitutions may change over time in ways that serve the interests of restricted subsets of society at the expense of the common interest, as represented by the substitution of rules and policies that emphasize the transfer of wealth for rules and policies that emphasize the creation of wealth.

Principles of Constitutional Political Economy

Constitutions form the basis for all social activity. Therefore, all economic production is ultimately a function of the constitutional order in place in a given society. Economists have traditionally maintained that production, in order to take place, requires some combination of three basic inputs: land (that is, all natural re-sources), labor, and capital (the result itself of a combination of land and labor over time). In fact, however, the constitution is another basic and vital "factor of production." The extent to which economic activity can be conducted efficiently is limited by the nature of the constitution. Regardless of the stock of labor and natural resources available within a country, the degree of freedom and economic opportunity available to its citizens and the rates of economic growth and development it is capable of achieving depend upon the constitutional constraints in place, for these govern the relative incentives of wealth-creating and wealth-transferring activities. There are many examples of unfree and undeveloped countries that have anemic economies but are nevertheless endowed with abundant labor, land, and natural resources (for example, the Soviet Union or the People's Republic of China), as well as of free, rapidly developing countries that have robust and energetic economies but meager endowments of natural resources and land (for example, Japan and Hong Kong). The difference in economic performance arises, to an important extent, because countries such as Japan have social constitutions that encourage and nurture freedom and economic opportunity for individual consumers and producers, whereas countries such as the People's Republic of China have constitutions that stifle and repress freedom and economic activity.

As previously noted, however, constitutions do not result from divine intervention. The same factor that dominates the determination of outcomes in private markets—the driving force of rational self-interest—is also the primary factor determining outcomes in constitutional "markets." Laws, conventions, and all other forms of social regulation are the outcome of the competition between various individuals, each seeking to maximize his or her own utility.

However, there is a vital difference between two kinds of constitutional competition. This difference reflects the fact that the social constitution can be separated into two fundamentally different parts. The first part is composed of those rules that are the result of a voluntary agreement between all participants; they are, in a strict sense, analogous to rules in sports. Everyone who plays baseball, for example, has agreed, of his or her own volition, to obey a certain set of rules of that game. Otherwise, they would not agree to play in the first place. The "voluntary" rules are the result of spontaneous agreement among all participants and represent a quite literal "social contract." As with ordinary contracts in private markets, no coercion is involved in securing agreement. Everyone involved agrees to abide by the rules in question because, in each individual case, they perceive themselves to be better off by so doing. Most customs, social conventions, and informal rules of social interaction—such as manners—are examples of the "sportslike" portion of the social constitution.

The other part of the constitution is determined and enforced through political processes. This includes laws, government regulations, and the actual, written constitution of the government in question. Unlike the "sportslike" portion of the constitution, this portion is not formulated as the result of completely voluntary agreement among all participants across free markets. Rather, it is the result of decisions made in the political sector and imposed on society whether all individuals agree or not. This portion of the constitution is based on coercion.

Despite this major distinction, the two portions of the constitution of a society are not, by their nature, fundamentally incompatible. The use of some coercion may be necessary in order to provide for the efficient operation—and even the existence—of a free society. For example, in the case of certain public goods, such as national defense, voluntary market exchange may not provide optimal quantities. A modification of the social constitution in such a way as to allow for a government to provide such necessary goods may represent an efficient solution. The protection of property rights by means of the formulation and enforcement of criminal law may be another similar example of a necessary governmental function requiring modifications to the social constitution in order to allow a certain and precisely delimited amount of coercion by government. Such forms of "coercive constitutionalism" may actually *increase* the level of individual liberty in society by protecting and extending the functioning of the free marketplace. Such coercive, political portions of the social constitution may form a necessary bulwark for a free market and a free society by serving to protect the rights of individuals from force and fraud.

However, there is another, darker side to the political constitution. What Caesar gives, Caesar can also take away. Because modifications to the political portion of the social constitution do not require the consent of all participants in the social order, modifications can occur that do not improve the welfare of all individuals. This is not the case with voluntary, "sportslike" constitutional rules: if changes in the rules did not benefit all participants, they would not voluntarily agree to those changes. But for changes in the political constitution, voluntary agreement on the part of all participants is irrelevant. Even if a large minority vigorously object to a given rule (whether statute, regulation, or other form), their objections are irrelevant so long as the measure in question has sufficient political support—in a democracy, a majority of the voters; in a nondemocracy, like most countries in the world today, perhaps much less—to ensure its passage. Those who object will simply be coerced into acceptance.

Hence, the major difference between the two types of constitutional change is obvious. Changes in the voluntary, spontaneous, "sportslike" constitution must, by definition, benefit all participants; otherwise, they would refuse to agree to the changes. By contrast, changes in the political portion of the constitution *do not* necessarily benefit all participants. They may benefit only the relatively small subset of society that is sufficient to ensure enactment of the changes, because the rest will be forced to accept them at the point of a gun. In both constitutional realms, individual actors are assumed to be rational and self-interested and to be seeking to maximize their own utility within a process in which they are competing with other individuals with similar motivations. The same economic principles describe the operation of competition in the market for rules with equal validity. The only important difference is that in the first realm, the competition is limited to the pursuit of voluntary agreement by means of persuading others; in the latter, competition extends to the use of force to provide the means to coerce compliance.

The Self-Ownership Foundations of a Democratic Polity

There is a logical dichotomy at the base of all discussions of political obligation that is very simple but that can be ignored only at our peril. It is an economic principle that all resources that have value are *owned* by someone. Extending this simple maxim to individuals provides the basis for this dichotomy: either individuals own themselves or someone else owns them.

The United States was founded on the premise—clearly expressed in both the Declaration of Independence and the Constitution—that each individual in society owns himself. This implies that individuals are free to pursue their own unique goals and, at the same time, that they are responsible for the consequences of their own actions. One of the most important of these responsibilities is respecting the equal freedom of other individuals to pursue their own ends similarly.

Other nations in the world today are founded on a different premise: that individuals do not own themselves but are, in effect, owned by the state. The state makes all important decisions regarding economic and social affairs, and individuals have no rights at all. Individuals have only the privileges that those who control the state deign to grant them, for as long as those in control find convenient.

Unfortunately, in the real world, the line of demarcation between these two extremes can become blurred. This is particularly the case in free societies with constitutions that have established democratic decision-making structures. There is a necessary tension between individual liberty and democracy that can tend to dilute the power of self-ownership of free individuals if it is not carefully controlled.

A free society does not necessarily require democratic governmental structures, but such structures are probably the best available for ensuring that the power of government is effectively constrained by the preferences of citizens. But democracy is like a fire. Carefully constrained and limited, it can be a valuable tool for accomplishing productive ends, as in clearing farmland of useless brush or in controlling floods. When it is not carefully constrained and limited, however, it can be immensely destructive of life, limb, and property.

Democracy only necessarily protects the freedom and property of the *majority*; without express protection, minority interests will be unprotected from the depredations of the majority. But even worse, the majority that is protected today may be a different group of people from that protected yesterday or that protected next week. In other words, majorities are not likely to be stable over time. This week, A and B may gang up on C and steal him blind; next week, B and C might do the same to A; and on and on. In the absence of effective constitutional constraints on the actions of government—bounds that clearly establish which uses of political coercion are legitimate and acceptable and which are illegitimate and unacceptable—democracy can be transformed from a useful social decision-making device to a kind of majoritarian tyranny based on the unrestrained hunt for plunder of vulnerable minority interests.

There is sometimes a tendency to use the term *democracy* as a synonym for *free society*. This is dangerously misleading. Even though free societies commonly find some variant of democratic decision making the most efficient means for controlling government, democracy in the absence of effective limits is just another form of tyranny.

The Founding Fathers worked long and hard on the thorny problem of how to establish a democratic form of government that would be effectively restrained from running roughshod over the rights of minorities (a term, as noted earlier, that refers to those unfortunate enough to be outside the majority coalition at the time in question). The U.S. Constitution was designed as a strong leash on a form of government that the Founding Fathers envisaged as a powerful, vicious dog—dangerous if allowed to roam free, but potentially an effective protector of the rights and property of the individuals who constitute the society.

Considerations from the Economic Theory of Legislation

As we saw in chapter 6, the modern economic theory of legislation has as its basis the fact that competition for legislation and regulation is affected by the same forces that affect competition across ordinary markets for other goods and services, and that the outcomes of political competition are as much the outcomes of market processes as those that flow from the ordinary, private marketplace. The same rational, self-interested, utility-maximizing individuals inhabit both worlds.

One implication of this analysis is that legislative outcomes normally tend to be the result of intense competition among competing interest groups that expect either to gain or to lose tangible and significant amounts of income from the passage (or nonpassage) of a law or regulation. In the real world, legislatures are unlikely to pass a law for the simple and altruistic reason that they expect that it will somehow make "society" better off. Legislatures typically act as a kind of brokerage firm, supplying wealth transfers to competing interest groups, thereby making some people in society better off at the expense of others.

It should be noted that this process of rent-seeking competition among interest groups is perfectly consistent with democracy. In one way or another, interest groups must purchase the votes of a majority in order to have the measures that benefit themselves passed. Democracy, by itself, places little constraint on the process of rent-seeking competition in the political sector, for it means only that policy measures must receive majority approval in a legislative assembly. However, it is fully possible for measures that would be rejected overwhelmingly in a referendum or plebiscite to receive majority approval in a legislature.

All political processes will necessarily be vulnerable to increasing control by rent-seeking interest groups unless there are effective constraints on what government coercion can be used to do and on what it is prohibited from doing. Otherwise, activity by government that reduces the welfare of society at large and tramples on the rights and liberties of individuals is not only possible but probable, if such activity would tend to benefit some interest group.

The political portion of the social constitution in general, not just laws passed by legislatures, will be determined in such an environment. Under ordinary circumstances, we should expect that changes are advocated in the political constitution of society primarily by groups that are seeking rents that they expect to flow to themselves as a result. Constitutions are a battlefield on which rent-seeking interest groups compete for coercive wealth transfers that they expect to result from the operation of the political process.

This has two major implications in terms of the constitution of society discussed here. First, any tendency toward shifting matters from the voluntary, "sportslike" constitutional arena to the political and coercive portion of the constitution will necessarily involve subjecting those matters to rent-seeking competition by interest groups that are striving for wealth transfers. Fantasies of disinterested, public-spirited politicians and regulators with a single-minded determination to enhance the welfare of society by enacting enlightened, legislation and regulation disintegrate after exposure to the real world. If government's power to intervene in society is kept tightly limited, this rent-seeking competition will be held in tight check as well. But in the absence of such constitutional limits on government, rent-seeking interest groups will almost inevitably come to dominate the process in their pursuit of wealth transfers. Second, although there is a natural tendency for matters left in the former realm to be resolved in a manner consistent with the rights and preferences of all, there is no such tendency in the latter. The former is the world of peaceful persuasion and cooperative competition; the latter is that of coercion and conflict.

Implications for Public Policy toward Tobacco

The implications of the constitutionalist perspective on social decision making for public policy with respect to tobacco products should also be obvious. As we have seen in chapters 3 through 5, there is no valid scientific basis for claiming that smokers impose costs on nonsmokers. In chapter 5, we saw that with respect to environmental tobacco smoke, there is no valid scientific basis for asserting that smokers impose uncompensated costs on nonsmokers. And in chapters 3 and 4, we saw that whatever harm smokers impose upon themselves by smoking is also borne economically by those smokers, not by nonsmokers.

Suppose that, sometime in the future, evidence becomes available that indicates that smoking seriously harms the health of *both* the smoker and those exposed to tobacco smoke in the environment. Would this fact make any difference in terms of restrictions by government on tobacco consumption by adults? Unless one is willing to reject the basis of the free society of self-owning and self-responsible individuals, it should not. Adults who smoke do so of their own free will and bear, voluntarily, whatever risks are associated with that activity. A case could always be made that smokers who do not understand the risks should be protected by government, because government possesses better information. However, such claims about knowledge seem far-fetched in the case of tobacco products. For twenty years, the federal government has engaged in a widely publicized, concerted campaign to convince the general public that smoking is dangerous. If there is any misinformation on the part of smokers, it is likely to be a substantially *exaggerated* idea of the riskiness of smoking, as we noted briefly in chapter 3. The same may be true for nonsmokers, many of whom may be nonsmokers *only* because the same informational bias leads them to hold exaggerated perceptions of the risks associated with smoking.

The fact remains that tobacco consumers smoke because the value they place on the benefits they receive from smoking exceeds the cost of smoking to them, including their perceived risk of health consequences. Similarly, nonsmokers who choose to expose themselves to ETS for extended periods do so because the benefits they receive from relationships with smokers exceed the costs of those relationships. To pretend that it is proper and necessary, in the case of either smokers or nonsmokers, for government to protect the public from cigarettes is tantamount to assuming that normal adults are incapable of making rational and coherent decisions regarding the conduct of their own lives. Even if smoking could be proved to generate significantly increased health risks either for smokers or for nonsmokers through ETS, mandatory restrictions on the behavior of smokers, ostensibly based on grounds of "protecting the public health," would imply that adult individuals in general were somehow unable to assess risks rationally and to make responsible decisions.

Of course, as we saw in chapter 6, political events do not just fall from the sky. Much antismoking rhetoric is likely to be rhetorical window-dressing, instrumental in the pursuit of rents through politics. Nonsmokers can be expected to gain higher wages as the result of clean indoor air acts at the expense of smokers, as the mandatory regulations act as a barrier to entry that generates monopoly rents. Politicians who view tax revenue as the raw material for wealth transfers that they can supply to favored interest groups will gain from the proceeds from tobacco taxes ostensibly enacted to improve the public health. Large restaurants may favor mandatory segregation of smokers and nonsmokers in order to impose relatively high costs on small restaurants, thereby reducing the competition they face. But whatever the real motivation behind the movement to restrict the consumption of tobacco products, it represents a fundamental rejection of the principles of individual liberty upon which a free society is ultimately founded.

Implications for Public Policy More Broadly Considered

If adults cannot be expected to make rational and responsible decisions about tobacco products without coercive government supervision, how can they be expected to make rational decisions concerning nutrition, child rearing, job selection, gardening, or house painting, among the myriad decisions they must make? Indeed, how can democracy be trusted to work well if people are such poor judges of their own self-interest? If government has the power to protect people from making choices that involve relatively high risks, why stop at tobacco consumption? What about skiing, mountain climbing, hang gliding, drinking alcohol, and working long hours? Are the risks "too high"? By whose standard? Some people are so risk-averse that they rarely venture out of their own homes.

As important as questions are involving the liberty of tobacco consumers to act on their free choice and mind their own business, there is another, much more important aspect to the tobacco question that extends far beyond cigarettes. Put simply, if government is going to be allowed to enact coercive measures that arbitrarily restrict the liberties and trample the rights of smokers, where will employment of this restrictive power end?

If government is not expressly prohibited from interfering with the free expression of voluntary choice by peaceful adults in the case of tobacco, what is to restrain the government from similarly imposing restrictions on political expression or religious practice? What is to prevent a conservative government from making liberal speech illegal, or vice versa? Sadly, the First Amendment to the Constitution may not be a sufficient answer. The First Amendment did not prevent the exclusion of tobacco advertising from television. The point is not that amendments to the written Constitution are necessarily without effect—surely, they can be vitally important—but rather than the one-time passage of such an amendment, no matter how stringent it sounds, may not be enough. If the general public is unwilling to oppose the tendency of the political sector, driven by the demands of rent-seeking interest groups, to expand beyond its necessary and proper domain, even a seemingly strong, written constitutional constraint enacted sometime in the past may prove ineffective.

If a broad social consensus exists that acquiesces to the legitimacy of governmental intrusions into the liberties and rights of individuals, further intrusions are much more likely. The liberty of all depends on drawing a line beyond which government may not cross. That line must represent the rejection by the general public of the principle of unlimited government intervention into the peaceful domain of social life. Tobacco regulation is only one example. Every time governmental power extends beyond the realm of the simple protection of individuals against force and fraud, the very existence of the free and competitive social order is increasingly threatened. Tobacco regulation may not itself constitute Pandora's box, but to the extent that the liberties of tobacco consumers are increasingly whittled away, the Pandora's box of statism is cracked open a little bit more.

References

Atkinson, Anthony B., and Townsend, Joy L. "Economic Aspects of Reduced Smoking." *Lancet* 3(1977): 492–95.

Blank, R.M., and Blinder, A.S. "Macroeconomics, Income Distribution, and Poverty." In J.H. Danziger and D.H. Weinberg (eds.), *Fighting Poverty: What Works and What Doesn't* (Cambridge, Mass.: Harvard University Press, 1986), pp. 180–208.

Boadway, Robin W. *Public Sector Economics* (Cambridge, Mass.: Winthrop, 1979).

Brennan, H. Geoffrey, and Buchanan, James M. *The Power to Tax* (Cambridge: Cambridge University Press, 1980).

Buchanan, James M. "The Economics of Earmarked Taxes" *Journal of Political Economy* 71(October 1963): 457–69.

———. *Cost and Choice* (Chicago: Markham, 1969).

———. "Politics and Meddlesome Preferences." In Robert D. Tollison (ed.), *Smoking and Society: Toward a More Balanced Assessment* (Lexington, Mass.: Lexington Books, 1986), pp. 335–42.

Buchanan, James M., and Tullock, Gordon. *The Calculus of Consent* (Ann Arbor: University of Michigan Press, 1962).

Coase, R.H. "The Problem of Social Cost." Journal of Law and Economics 3(October 1960): 1–44.

Committee on Ways and Means. *Hearings on User Fees, Revenue Proposals Contained in President Reagan's 1986 Budget, and Other Revenue Measures* (Washington, D.C.: U.S. Government Printing Office, 1986).

Cowell, M.J., and Hirst, B.L. "Mortality Differences between Smokers and Nonsmokers." *Transactions of the Society of Actuaries* 32(1980): 185–261.

Dahl, Tor; Gunderson, Barbara; and Kuehnast, Kathleen. "The Influence of Health Improvement Programs on White Collar Productivity." Working paper, University of Minnesota, Minneapolis, 1984.

Danziger, S.H., and Gottschalk, P. "The Impact of Budget Cuts and Economic Conditions on Poverty." *Journal of Policy Analysis and Management* 5(1985): 587–93.

Den Uyl, Douglas J. "Smoking, Human Rights, and Civil Liberties." In Robert D. Tollison (ed.), *Smoking and Society: Toward a More Balanced Assessment* (Lexington, Mass.: Lexington Books, 1986), pp. 189–216.

Doll, Richard, and Peto, Richard. "The Causes of Cancer: Quantitative Estimates of Avoidable Risks of Cancer in the United States Today." *Journal of the National Cancer Institute* 66(June 1981): 1193–1308.

Efron, Edith. *The Apocalyptics: Cancer and the Big Lie* (New York: Simon and Schuster, 1984).

Egger, Garry. "Increasing Health Costs from Smoking." Health Commission of New South Wales, Australia, May 1978.

Epstein, Richard A. *Taxings: Private Property and the Power of Eminent Domain* (Cambridge: Harvard University Press, 1985).

Ferrara, Peter J. *Social Security: The Inherent Contradiction* (Washington, D.C.: Cato Institute, 1980).

Hammond, E.C. "Smoking in Relation to the Death Rates of One Million Men and Women." In *Epidemiological Study of Cancer and Other Chronic Diseases,* National Cancer Institute Monograph No. 19 (Washington, D.C.: U.S. Government Printing Office, 1966), pp. 127–204.

Holcomb, Harry S., III, and Meigs, J. Wister. "Medical Absenteeism among Cigarette, Cigar, and Pipe Smokers." *Archives of Environmental Health* 25(October 1972): 295–300.

Kristein, Marvin M. "Economic Issues in Prevention," *Preventive Medicine* 6(1977): 252–64.

Lee, Dwight R., and Tollison, Robert D. "Towards a True Measure of Excess Burden." Working paper, Center for Study of Public Choice, Fairfax, Va., 1985.

Leu, Robert E. "Anti-Smoking Publicity, Taxation, and the Demand for Cigarettes." *Journal of Health Economics* 3(1984): 101–16.

Leu, Robert E., and Schaub, Thomas. "Does Smoking Increase Medical Care Expenditure?" *Social Science and Medicine* 17(1983): 1907–14.

Lewit, E.M., and Coate, D. "The Potential for Using Excise Taxes to Reduce Smoking," *Journal of Health Economics* 1(1982): 121–45.

Luce, Bryan R., and Schweitzer, Stuart O., "The Economic Costs of Smoking-Induced Illness," National Institute of Drug Abuse Research Monograph Series, No. 7, Department of Health, Education, and Welfare, December 1977.

———. "Smoking and Alcohol Abuse: A Comparison of Their Economic Consequences." *New England Journal of Medicine,* 9 March 1978, 569–71.

McCormick, Robert E., and Tollison, Robert D., *Politicians, Legislation, and the Economy* (Boston: Martinus Nijhoff, 1981).

McMahon, Walter W., and Sprenkle, Case M. "A Theory of Earmarking." *National Tax Journal* 23(September 1970): 255–61.

Minarik, Joseph J. *Making Tax Choices* (Washington, D.C.: Urban Institute Press, 1985).

Musgrave, Richard A. *The Theory of Public Finance* (New York: McGraw-Hill, 1959).

National Research Council, Committee on Passive Smoking, Board on Environmental Studies and Toxicology. *Environmental Tobacco Smoke: Measuring Exposures and Assessing Health Effects* (Washington, D.C.: National Academy Press, 1986).

Niskanen, William A. Jr. *Bureaucracy and Representative Government.* (Chicago: Aldine-Atherton, 1971).

Office of Management and Budget. *Budget of the United States Government, Fiscal 1985* (Washington, D.C.: U.S. Government Printing Office, 1984).

Office of Technology Assessment Staff Memorandum. *Smoking-Related Deaths and Financial Costs.* (Washington, D.C.: Office of Technology Assessment, 1985).

Oster, Gerry; Colditz, Graham A.; and Kelly, Nancy L. *The Economic Costs of Smoking and Benefits of Quitting* (Lexington, Mass.: Lexington Books, 1984).

Pechman, Joseph A. *Who Pays the Taxes?* (Washington, D.C.: Brookings Institution, 1985).

Peltzman, Sam. "Constituent Interest and Congressional Voting." *Journal of Law and Economics* 27(April 1984): 181–210.

Peston, M.H. "Economics and Cigarette Smoking." *The Second World Conference on Smoking and Health:* Proceedings of a Conference Organized by the Health Education Council (R. Richardson Editor) (Empirial College of London: London, England, 1971).

Ravenholt, R.T. "Addiction Mortality in the United States, 1980: Tobacco, Alcohol, and Other Substances." *Population and Development Review* 10(December 1984): 697–724.

Robertson, A. Haeworth. *The Coming Revolution in Social Security* (Reston, Va.: Reston, 1981).

Seltzer, Carl C. "Smoking and Coronary Heart Disease: What Are We to Believe?" *American Heart Journal* 100(September 1980): 275–80.

Shillington, E. Richard. *Selected Economic Consequences of Cigarette Smoking* (Ottawa, Canada: National Ministry of Health and Welfare, 1977).

Shughart, William F., II, and Savarese, James M. "The Incidence of Taxes on Tobacco." In Robert D. Tollison (ed.), *Smoking and Society: Toward a More Balanced Assessment* (Lexington, Mass.: Lexington Books, 1986), pp. 285–307.

Shughart, William F., II, and Tollison, Robert D. "Smokers versus Nonsmokers." In Robert D. Tollison (ed.), *Smoking and Society: Toward a More Balanced Assessment* (Lexington, Mass.: Lexington Books, 1986), pp. 217–24.

Solmon, Lewis C. "The Other Side of the Smoking Worker Controversy." *Personnel Administrator* 28(March 1983): 72ff.

Spielberger, Charles D. "Psychological Determinants of Smoking Behavior." In Robert D. Tollison (ed.), *Smoking and Society: Toward a More Balanced Assessment* (Lexington, Mass.: Lexington Books, 1966), pp. 89–134.

Sterling, T., and Weinkam, J. "Smoking Characteristics by Type of Employment." *Journal of Occupational Medicine* 18(1976): 743–54.

Stoddart, Greg L., et al. "Tobacco Taxes and Health Care Costs: Do Canadian Smokers Pay Their Way?" *Journal of Health Economics* 5(1986): 63–80.

Survey of Businesses and Eating Establishments in Montgomery County, Maryland. Hamilton and Associates, 1982.

Szasz, Thomas. *The Theology of Medicine* (New York: Colophon Books, 1978).

Taylor, Daniel T. "Absent Workers and Lost Work Hours, May 1978." *Monthly Labor Review* 102(August 1979): 49–53.

Tobacco Institute. *The Tax Burden on Tobacco, Vol. 19, 1984* (Washington: Tobacco Institute, 1985).

Tullock, Gordon. *The Politics of Bureaucracy.* (Washington, D.C.: Public Affairs Press, 1965).

U.S. Department of Labor, Bureau of Labor Statistics. *Consumer Expenditure Survey: Diary Survey, 1980–81.* (Washington, D.C.: U.S. Government Printing Office, September 1983).

Vogel, Alfred. "Are Smokers Really Less Productive than Nonsmokers?" *Legislative Policy,* Summer 1985, 6–8.

Wagner, Richard E. *Public Finance: Revenues and Expenditures in a Democratic Society* (Boston: Little, Brown, 1983).

Weaver, Carolyn L. *The Crisis in Social Security: Economic and Political Origins* (Durham, N.C.: Duke University Press, 1982).

Index

About the Authors

Robert D. Tollison is professor of economics and director of the Center for Study of Public Choice at George Mason University in Fairfax, Virginia. He has published more than two hundred articles in professional economics journals and authored or edited some thirteen books including *Smoking and Society* and *Clearing the Air,* published by Lexington Books. He is a former director of the Bureau of Economics at the Federal Trade Commission and a past president of the Southern Economic Association. He is also the coauthor (with R.B. Ekelund, Jr.) of *Economics,* a best-selling economics textbook for college students.

Richard E. Wagner is professor of economics at George Mason University in Fairfax, Virginia. He received a B.S. from the University of Southern California and received his Ph.D. from the University of Virginia. He has been on the faculties of Auburn University, Virginia Polytechnic Institute and State University, Tulane University, and the University of California at Irvine, as well as a visiting professor at the University of Konstanz. Among the books he has authored are *The Fiscal Organization of American Federalism, The Public Economy, Inheritance and the State,* and *Democracy in Deficit* (with James M. Buchanan). He has also authored numerous articles in books and journals. His current research interests include constitutional law and economics and corporate models of governance.